The Brain Sharpeners Abroad

Andersen Young Readers' Library

PHILIP CURTIS

The Brain
Sharpeners
Abroad

Illustrated by Tony Ross

Andersen Press · London

First published in 1987 by
Andersen Press Limited,
62-65 Chandos Place,
London WC2

British Library Cataloguing in Publication Data
Curtis, Philip
  The brain sharpeners abroad.—
  (Andersen young readers' library).
  I. Title   II. Ross, Tony
  823'.914[J]   PZ7

ISBN 0-86264-183-7

Printed and bound in Great Britain by
Anchor Brendon Limited, Tiptree, Essex

Contents

1

Class 8 on the Continent

'I know something that you don't,' said Inga Somervil to Spiky Jackson, who had been annoying her by knocking her hopscotch markers out of position and generally interfering with the playtime game.

'If you know it and I don't, then it can't be worth knowing,' replied Spiky, sitting down on the nearest bench along the edge of the playground.

'What a nerve he has!' called out Anna Cardwell as she hopped among the squares. 'I wouldn't bother to tell him, Inga, he's just a pest!'

'Do you know what it is she knows, Anna?' asked Spiky, trying not to show the slightest curiosity.

'No, she doesn't,' replied Inga. 'I don't suppose even Mr Browser knows, yet. Maybe the Headmaster, does, though. Yes, I think he must do. My mum's coming up to school to talk to him about it later on this morning.'

'Watch out, Spiky, you could be in trouble!' chimed in Michael Fairlie, who was on the same bench as Spiky, reading a comic. 'What's he been up to, Inga?'

'It's nothing to do with him—yet,' replied Inga, enjoying the growing mystery she had created. 'But it could be soon—and to do with you, Michael, and with most of the class.'

'Who cares!' said Spiky. 'Give me a page of your comic, Mike. It's more and more boring round here.'

'You can have the whole thing,' declared Michael. 'I'm going to have a drink of water.'

He stood up to go to the water tap in the cloakroom, and Inga realised that she was in danger of losing her whole audience.

'Are you going anywhere in the Whitsun holiday, Spiky?' she asked.

'Me? No—what's that to do with it?'

'A great deal. You might be going somewhere, you see, if your mum and dad agree. And so might you, Michael—and Anna.'

Anna stopped hopping, Michael turned back and Spiky put down the comic. Inga had all the attention she wanted.

'Out with it, or—' began Spiky.

'My mum's trying to arrange for Class 8 to go to Germany this Whitsun, and stay with children from her old school,' announced Inga.

This was news for thought, but Spiky didn't much like to be caught unprepared.

'I don't suppose Sage will agree,' he said. 'Besides, it would cost too much.'

'No it won't—we'd only have to pay the fare, because we'd live with families over there. My mum knows the Head of the school over there. She's talked

8

to him on the phone, and he's agreed.'

'I still don't think Sage will do it—and I'm sure old Browser won't want to spend Whitsun with us!' declared Spiky, his last words almost drowned by the piercing note of Mr Caracco's whistle announcing that playtime had ended. They all stood still.

'You just wait and see!' said Inga, determined to enjoy her moments of importance to the full.

'Quiet!' shouted Mr Caracco. 'Class 8, lead in!'

As Class 8 formed a line along the path leading into school, a plump, fair-haired lady walked briskly up the path from the direction of the school gate.

'I told you! There she is,' whispered Inga. No reply was possible, for Mr Sage was standing at the door to make sure that silence was maintained.

'Good morning, Mrs Somervil,' he greeted the chubby lady. 'Please make your way to my room. I'll be with you in a moment.'

Mrs Inge Somervil walked into the school, greeted Miss Copewell the secretary and then sat down in Mr Sage's room. She spelt her own name, Inge, with an 'e' at the end of it, as is usual in Germany, but she had insisted that her daughter be christened Inga with an 'a', as if to emphasise that she had been born in England. Inga's father held a very important position with the council, but he wasn't half as busy as his wife, who very quickly after her arrival at Chivvy Chase became a governor of the school, and rather worried

9

Mr Sage with her many ideas to improve it.

She was also the one who urged her husband to persuade the councillors that Chivvy Chase should be 'twinned' with her home town of Bad Unterfeld, and now she was set on linking her own old school with her daughter's.

'It's no good,' she said to Mr Sage, 'just putting notices up on the road signs to say that we're twinned with Bad Unterfeld, and then doing nothing about it, which seems to be the council's idea. Let the children of each town get to know each other and at least we'll be doing something for international understanding.'

'Yes, but—' said Mr Sage, and he said that a number of times, but each time Inge Somervil had an answer for him. In the end, perhaps because Mr Somervil was rather an important man, Mr Sage was persuaded that a visit by Class 8 to Bad Unterfeld would be just the thing.

'Mr Browser speaks some German,' he said. 'I'll have a word with him.'

'Excellent,' said Mrs Somervil, standing up. 'Now I must go and organise the Women's Institute Jumble Sale. I'll telephone Herr Weissmann, the head of the school, this evening, and we can start making arrangements—'

'Hold on!' protested Mr Sage. 'I'll have to make sure enough teachers and children want to go, first of all.'

'Oh, I'm sure they will!' declared Mrs Somervil. 'What an opportunity! The children will love it.'

So Mr Sage came into Class 8's room and interrupted Mr Browser's lesson on the hopfields of Kent, one which he rather enjoyed.

'How about a class visit to Germany this Whitsun?' began Mr Sage, and explained everything just as he'd had it all explained to him.

'Yes, but—' put in Mr Browser, and told Mr Sage

that he really didn't speak much German—and what about the insurance—and weren't the children too young to go—and would enough adults want to go? Mr Sage knew the answers to all these questions, because he had just been given them by Mrs Somervil.

Spiky and Michael Fairlie, sitting in the group at the front, pretended to draw an oast house in Kent, but heard enough to realise that a visit was being discussed.

'Inga was right,' said Spiky afterwards. 'Do you want to go, Mike?'

'Why not?' answered Mike. 'It depends on what sort of place this Bad—whatever it is—turns out to be.'

'Who wants to go to a place called bad?' observed Spiky.

But Mrs Somervil was not to be stopped, and in a short time all was arranged. Spiky discovered that 'Bad' means the same as 'Spa', and that Bad Unterfeld was a pleasant little place surrounded by woods. Inga's mother came and gave a little talk about it, and told them about the pleasant countryside and how the delights of the open air swimming pool made the Chivvy Chase one look old-fashioned. Mr Browser busied himself with a book on German conversation, just to remind himself of what he once knew, and Mr Caracco agreed to go with the party if he could bring his guitar. Mr Sage couldn't come because he had an important meeting to attend in the holiday.

Inga and Spiky and Michael and Anna and the rest of those whose parents had allowed them to go on the visit had no idea of all the hustle and bustle which Mrs Somervil and Mr Browser and Mr Caracco had to endure before the arrangements were completed.

All they knew was that a few weeks later they were waving goodbye to their parents at Chivvy Chase station and heading for the night ferry from Harwich to the Hook of Holland. The boat was like a floating hotel, but Class 8 were not allowed to see much of it. They were fussed into their bunks by Inga's mother and Mr Browser, with Mr Caracco hovering around trying to look useful. Spiky was lucky—he could see the coast disappearing as the ship left harbour, because his cabin, shared with Michael, Selwyn and Jason Little, had a porthole. The rest, not so fortunate, were lulled to sleep by the engine sounds, and Spiky fell asleep soon afterwards.

He awoke to find that land was still in sight, but now it was coming nearer every minute.

'Wake up, Mike!' he called. 'We're in Holland!'

'Looks just like England,' was Mike's sleepy verdict.

Very soon the teachers and Mrs Somervil were making their rounds, and shepherded the party on the deck.

'I'm hungry!' complained Spiky.

'Breakfast will be taken on the train,' said Mrs

13

Somervil. 'Make sure that you have all your luggage, and keep with your teachers. Everybody ready?'

She was answered by tired yawns and one or two groans. They moved off the boat at a smart pace, then along a platform and into a waiting train. Breakfast consisted of rolls and butter and jam and cold meats, and this didn't meet with the approval of everyone.

'It's the same in Austria,' said Spiky knowledgeably. 'Might as well get used to it. You're not eating, Anna. I'll have yours, if you like—'

To his surprise Anna Cardwell nodded her agreement. She looked pale and uneasy.

'What's the matter, Anna?' asked her friend Alison.

'I had a bad dream,' said Anna.

'What about?' asked Spiky, munching her roll.

'I dreamt—that creatures were warning us off, telling us not to go to Bad Unterfeld,' said Anna. Mrs Somervil came by, urging children to eat and drink.

'Creatures, Anna? What creatures?' she asked. 'You'll feel better if you eat something, Anna. Maybe the voyage didn't suit you. Don't worry, you're on dry land now, and you surely can't be homesick already.'

She moved on, not really interested in Anna's dream creatures.

'It wasn't the sea,' said Anna. 'Those creatures were warning us, I'm sure.'

'Don't talk nonsense, Anna,' said Inga, who was naturally anxious that the whole visit should be

14

a success.

'What were they like, Anna?' asked Selwyn.

'Like? They had very big heads and large eyes, and they scared me just by looking at me. That's it—the way they looked at me reminded me of—of the Brain Sharpeners!'

'Brain Sharpeners?' It was a long time since these words had been spoken, and Spiky and Selwyn looked uneasy, as though their continental coffee disagreed with them. Inga, who had been away from school ill for some weeks during the year, could dismiss the idea with a laugh, and Alison tried to cheer her friend up.

'It's all that chocolate you ate on the train yesterday,' she suggested. 'Or else you really are homesick—'

'Of course not!' protested Anna, and drank some hot coffee.

'Look—I can see a couple of windmills,' said Inga. 'And what a crowd of cyclists at the level crossing!'

'It's as flat as a pancake here,' observed Spiky. 'I like Chivvy Chase better. At least there are one or two hills to climb.'

'Oh, there are in Bad Unterfeld too,' said Inga.

They watched the fields and the windmills and the cyclists as the Dutch countryside was crossed at great speed.

'We're near the border now,' Inga informed them. 'I've been on this journey lots of times before.'

15

She was right. The train slowed down and customs men in different uniforms passed along the corridor. Finally the train stopped, only to start up again with a sudden jolt and put on speed as it entered Germany.

They were silent as they stared at the streets of the small border town, as if they expected something strange to happen.

'It looks just the same to me,' said Spiky. 'You couldn't tell which country you were in if it hadn't been for the customs men.'

'It is the same,' said Inga. 'It won't change for a while yet, and then there'll be hills and woods.'

'How much longer is it, Mr Browser?' asked Spiky as Mr Browser lurched along the corridor.

'About two hours more on this train, then we change to a local one and travel for an hour on that,' replied Mr Browser. 'We eat lunch when we change trains, if that's what you're worried about. Everyone all right?'

'Yes, thank you,' said Alison. 'Anna's eaten a couple of my sandwiches, and she's feeling better now.'

'I never felt unwell,' grumbled Anna when Mr Browser had gone.

The train at last drew into a junction as if exhausted, and the children were all pleased to step out on the platform and walk up and down while Mrs Somervil arranged for them to eat in the station restaurant.

The meal, especially the ice cream and cool orange juice, was generally approved of, as the empty plates showed.

'Over the bridge to platform three,' announced Mr Browser afterwards. 'Next stop, Bad Unterfeld. When we arrive there, the teachers and children of the Franz Schubert School will be there to meet you. They'll take you to the school and there you'll be paired up with the boy or girl you're staying with. You'll no doubt get to know them on the way to the school, as you already know their names.'

The local train was in no hurry as it trundled along, but the scenery was more interesting than any they'd seen that day. There were wide fields of growing corn, mixed with blocks of dark pine woods, and in the background were hills covered with patches of forest, as though someone with a huge mower had chopped away some parts and left the others. The clouds sent shadows flying across the treeless parts, and then the sun would turn them green again.

Mrs Somervil was becoming very excited.

'Bad Unterfeld,' she called out as she sped along the corridor, poking her head into each compartment. 'Make sure you have everything ready.'

Spiky Jackson found time to look out of the window as the train drew into the platform.

'Cor! Mike—they've brought a band to welcome us!' he said, withdrawing his head from the window

17

and picking up his luggage. Class 8 stumbled, jumped and almost fell off the train, surprised by the height of the step above the platform.

'Gather round me!' called out Inga's mother, keen as a sheepdog to bring them together. 'Make four lines and put your luggage down.'

Mr Browser could have told her that in such circumstances making two lines was hard enough. Trying to make four led to a confused group milling about and falling over their own belongings. Mrs Somervil was just becoming frantic when the town band saved the situation by suddenly striking up. The band consisted chiefly of silver-haired gentlemen, and it was playing a tune which Mr Browser recognised as 'It's a long way to Tipperary'. Standing in a group behind the band were the Stationmaster, in a handsome cap and uniform, and the representatives of the Franz Schubert School—several adults and a group of children.

Everybody struggled to keep their balance and stand still, and when the band finished Mrs Somervil stepped forward and led the applause. Then a man stepped forward from behind the band. He was thin, with wavy silvery hair, and he wore steel-rimmed glasses behind which were blue, twinkling eyes.

'Herr Weissmann!' said Mrs Somervil, moving forward to greet him. 'We have arrived!'

'It is my pleasure,' said the Headmaster, 'to welcome you all to Bad Unterfeld and the Franz Schubert School. 'We all hope—'

'Whoooosh!' went the engine, and he had to wait until the train, which had remained to enjoy the music—or because Bad Unterfeld was a small junction—had clanked out of the station.

'We all hope you will have a most excellent time, enjoying yourselves and making good friends. Oh dear, what is the matter with that little girl? Frau Somervil, she looks so white—'

Mrs Somervil turned to see Anna, her face pale as death, swaying on her feet. Her friend Alison saw Herr Weissmann's blue eyes on her friend, and grabbed her in time to save her from falling.

'What's the matter, Anna?' she asked.

'It was the Brain Sharpeners,' mumbled Anna. 'He's in their power—I can see it in his eyes!'

'In whose eyes?' asked Alison—but she received no reply. Anna had fainted.

'Oh dear, oh dear,' said Mrs Somervil as Miss Copewell tried to bring her round. 'The sea trip didn't agree with her, I'm afraid. And she's hardly had anything to eat.'

'Poor child,' said Herr Weissmann. 'We will order for her a taxi—'

'That's all right,' said Miss Copewell. 'We'll look after her. Is it far to the school, Mrs Somervil?'

'Only a few metres down the road,' replied that

19

lady. 'We can carry her that far, if necessary. Stand back, the rest of you, and let her have some fresh air. I think she's coming round.'

'Then let us depart,' said Herr Weissmann. 'The rest of the children are waiting at the school to meet their new friends. We did not want to overcrowd the station. Please follow me, ladies and gentlemen, and children.'

The magnificent Stationmaster made a little bow, the band picked up their instruments and were thanked, and Herr Weissmann led on proudly towards his school.

Anna struggled to her feet, and protested that she was now perfectly all right, and could walk on her own.

'Never mind, Anna, the journey is soon over,' said Mrs Somervil.

'What made you faint, Anna?' asked Alison.

'It was that man, the Headmaster,' whispered Anna. 'I saw someone just like him in my dream about the Brain Sharpeners!'

'That dream! Something must have badly disagreed with you,' said Alison, but Anna shook her head.

'Welcome to Franz Schubert School,' said Herr Weissmann, and directed them into the playground of his school, which was built of large, old, grey stone blocks, which looked ready to stand for another hundred years.

'It makes Chivvy Chase look modern,' was Spiky's verdict. 'But I bet it lasts longer,' he added as they passed between the heavy entrance doors into a highly polished entrance hall. A dark-haired young lady teacher was waiting to receive them.

'This is Fräulein Schmidt,' said Herr Weissmann.

'She is the teacher of Class S, who will be hosts to Class 8 for their visit.'

'Please come this way,' said Fräulein Schmidt.

'A very good class, Class S,' observed Herr Weissmann as they followed her. 'Very hard workers indeed. Clever too. Improving each day, it seems.' His eyes twinkled behind his glasses.

'I bet they're clever,' whispered Anna, 'I was afraid of that.'

'Why?' asked Alison—but there was no time to reply.

'Come along, children,' Mrs Somervil urged them. 'Now you will meet your new friends.'

2

Spiky and Helmut

In Fräulein Schmidt's classroom the rest of Class S were waiting with all the parents, ready to play hosts to Class 8. Herr Weissmann couldn't resist making another little speech, to which Mr Browser replied, but neither the English nor the German children appeared to be listening. They were far more concerned with trying to decide with whom they were to be matched. At last Herr Weissmann could delay the moments of introduction no longer.

'I will now call upon Miss Schmidt to read out the names of the children who are to be together,' he said in English, and then spoke somewhat more rapidly in German. Fräulein Schmidt, whose face was now half hidden behind giant tortoiseshell glasses, stood up with a piece of paper in her hand.

'Alison Gilpin—Martel Kaufman.'

Martel stood up, and Alison moved across to join her and her mother.

'Anna Cardwell—Astrid Bertram.'

The girls were being paired off first, and Spiky eyed up the selection of possible boys suspiciously. It was going to be a matter of great importance, he suddenly realised, with which of these boys his fate was to be linked for the next week. There were fattish ones, thin ones, sporting looking ones and studious types—and he prayed that he might be spared the company of one of these!

'Simon Yackson—Helmut Schneider.'

'Yackson—that's you, Spiky,' whispered Mike, giving him a nudge.

'Simon Jackson,' said Mrs Somervil, and Fräulein Schmidt blushed.

'Oh dear, my English! Simon Jackson, of course,' she corrected herself.

'Don't worry—your English is excellent,' declared Mr Caracco, and Fräulein Schmidt blushed again.

A stolid boy with a short back and sides haircut had stood up, and Spiky had time to reflect that his fate could have been worse before he had to shake hands with Helmut and his pale-faced mother.

The pairing went on until all the visitors had been allotted to families. The children stood there rather like sheep which have been rounded up and aren't sure what is going to happen to them, and the scene was so serious that Mr Caracco felt obliged to wink at some of them and Mr Browser tried to smile. Inga's mother was happiest of all, because all her plans were becoming reality.

'Before you all go home,' she said, 'there are one or two things I'd like to tell you.'

If the children of Mr Browser's class were not aware

of it, or had forgotten, they were unpleasantly reminded by Mrs Somervil that the children of Franz
Schubert School had finished their Whitsun holiday
the previous week, and therefore would be reporting
to school at eight o'clock the next day—and the
English visitors would come with them. There would
be a short tour of the town for Class 8 in the morning,
then the afternoon would be free, as the Franz Schu-

bert School finished work at one o'clock.

'Eight o'clock!' muttered Spiky to Selwyn, who was standing beside him. 'That means being up at seven. Call it a holiday!'

'Finished at one, though,' Selwyn whispered back. 'Plenty of the day left.'

'For you,' put in Helmut in slow English. 'For us, there is the homework.'

'You speak English!' said Spiky, much relieved.

'A little. I have learned very much in the three weeks up to today.'

'Not bad for three weeks,' said Spiky. 'Mr Browser has been trying to teach us German—but all I can remember is *danke schön*.'

'I am now a very good learner,' said Helmut. 'It was not always so. Now we are all very good learners in Class S.'

'It is because Herr Weissmann now takes the class very much,' said the boy who was Selwyn's partner. He was a very earnest, pale boy of a studious type, clearly chosen at the suggestion of Mrs Somervil as the right type for Selwyn.

'To come to school will not be a problem for you,' said Helmut to Spiky. 'My father is a policeman, and he has no duty tomorrow, so he will bring me and you in his car.'

It didn't occur to Spiky to think that Mrs Somervil might have considered it a good idea to place him under the control of a policeman; he was one of those modest boys who think that any troubles they have are not of their own making.

Soon Mrs Somervil had said all she wanted to for the moment. If any of the girls were in trouble, the family concerned should telephone her at her home; if a boy had a problem—or was a problem—Mr Browser was to be rung at the home of the Headmaster, where he would be staying. The gathering then broke up, and the families departed with their visitors, sent on their way with a satisfied smile from the Headmaster.

Spiky and Helmut trailed around after Helmut's mother, who had to do some shopping in a supermarket very much like one of those at Chivvy Chase. With some difficulty Helmut discovered something which Spiky would like to eat, and after a walk of about half a mile they turned up a street which Helmut declared to be his.

'Kramer Strasse 127 is where we live,' he said. 'Don't forget that, Simon, in case you go out alone.'

'127 Kramer Strasse,' repeated Spiky. 'Call me Spiky,' he added. 'Everybody in my class does.'

Mrs Schneider let herself in to a neat new terrace house. She was a rather floppy lady, whose pale complexion made her look younger than she was, so that Spiky was surprised by her lack of energy. Shopping had evidently tired her, and she soon disappeared into her bedroom, after telling Helmut to show Spiky his pet rabbit in the garden. To Spiky's relief, the policeman was not there; Spiky had much respect for policemen, but the thought of living in the same house as a foreign one—who probably would be carrying a gun—turned that respect almost into fear. He listened to Helmut's description of his rabbit, his bicycle and some of his toys as attentively as he could, considering he was all the time awaiting the arrival of Herr Schneider.

Helmut, meanwhile, turned out to be a friendly kind of boy who looked ordinary enough but possessed an extraordinary store of knowledge. He had learned much lately about England, he said. Did Spiky know the height of St. Paul's Cathedral, for example?

'I haven't a clue,' said Spiky.

'You mean you do not know. It is three hundred and sixty-five feet high, one foot for each day of the year.'

'Is it?' responded Spiky.

'Yes. That is nothing when you think about the Empire State Building in New York. That is one thousand two hundred and fifty feet high.'

'Indeed? How high is your house?' asked Spiky. Helmut was only put off for a second.

'I will ask my father to look at the measurements,' he said. 'He will tell you very quickly.'

29

'Don't worry,' said Spiky, who was beginning to be somewhat worried himself. Could he live peacefully with this human encyclopedia for a whole long week? Uneasy memories of a time when he had developed a strange wish to study and do nothing else returned vaguely to him, but he put these thoughts away from him and tried to do justice to himself when answering Helmut's many questions.

'What do you like to be when you grow up?' asked Helmut, looking critically at Spiky.

'Oh, I don't know. Perhaps a fireman,' replied Spiky. Helmut gave him a superior smile.

'I did want to be a policeman, like my father,' he said. 'But lately since I have studied so hard, I think I will become a professor.'

'Professor of what?' asked Spiky, hoping to bring Helmut down to earth.

'Professor of whatever subject I like to study,' replied Helmut. 'I'm pretty clever at the *Mathematik* at the moment.' Spiky said no more.

Some time later Frau Schneider came down from upstairs with sleepy eyes, and began to spread cooking smells throughout the house.

'Let us go and look at my homework books,' said Helmut, and they went to his bedroom. Spiky looked at the books, but they were in German and appeared to be much more difficult than his own school work, especially the maths, and he was grateful when Helmut was interrupted by the sound of a car drawing up outside the house.'

'My father,' said Helmut, and they went to the window.

The police car was green, and the man who stepped out of it was wearing a greenish uniform. From the moment he stepped from the car all Spiky's anxiety died away; Herr Schneider was a stocky man with dark hair combed straight back like Helmut's was, and his friendly wave to the two of them at the window was enough to put Spiky at ease.

The policeman, too, was quick to be at ease at home. He flung off his jacket, sang as he had a wash and joined them cheerfully for the evening meal. Spiky found the soup sharp and the meat fatty, but fortunately he enjoyed salad, and ate the large side plate of it with a good appetite.

'My English is not good like Helmut's,' he said. 'You think you can be friendly together?'

'Of course,' said Spiky politely.

'He is a good boy,' said the policeman, patting Helmut's shoulder. 'Very quickly he has become too clever for me, but I think that must be good, yes?'

'I suppose so,' agreed Spiky, realising that Herr Schneider was not quite sure.

'For three weeks, he only studies,' said the policeman. 'He has—you say, changed himself. Before, he like sport, running, jumping, swinging on the poles—

but now, he is too clever for that. He knows more than this policeman now! That Herr Weissmann, he is a very clever man. He has done much to my son, and to all those in his class. It is a wonder, I think.'

'A miracle,' Helmut corrected him.

Frau Schneider said something in German, and as she spoke alarm bells were ringing inside Spiky's head. So Helmut had suddenly changed, and the Headmaster had done it. He remembered how Anna had fainted on the station, and explained how she had seen Herr Weissmann in her dream—along with the Brain Sharpeners.

The Brain Sharpeners! Could it be that they were still trying to capture children for their colonising plans? Having failed in England, did they think that Germany might be fruitful ground? Or was all this sudden cleverness a normal happening?

'My wife says she is proud that Helmut is becoming clever. It is good to have one clever person in the family, she says.'

'I don't know—it depends,' said Spiky, eating up his mousse-like pudding.

'What do you mean, depends?' asked Helmut.

'Oh, I didn't mean anything,' said Spiky hastily, and Helmut gave him a superior glance.

'Cleverness is the most important thing,' he said.

'Shall we watch a programme—there is a football match coming soon?' said Herr Schneider.

'Oh, yes, I'd like to,' replied Spiky.

'You two can watch—I shall do my studying,' declared Helmut, and went to his bedroom.

'What a clever boy,' said Frau Schneider, spilling some coffee on the table as she collected up the plates. 'He will become something very big, I know that.'

Spiky couldn't understand what she had said, but her proud look told him everything. While he watched the football match, memories of the threat of the Brain Sharpeners when they had come to Chivvy Chase School flooded back to him. They didn't last long, and he didn't want to dwell on them, because it had been a painful time when the Brain Sharpeners had tried to claim him, and only Michael Fairlie had saved the class from transportation into space. It seemed unlikely to him that the Brain Sharpeners could have returned to attempt the same sort of conquest with some German children in a little town almost hidden by woods and hills. Besides, he was becoming tired after the long day's travel and the strain of making friends with people who had difficulty in making themselves understood in his own language. He should give thanks for Helmut's cleverness, he decided, not try to create problems about it.

The evening ended in general friendliness and the drinking of a pleasant fruit drink. Helmut showed him to a clean little bedroom with a comfortable bed.

34

'Goodnight, Simon,' said Helmut, who couldn't yet bring himself to say 'Spiky' because that clearly wasn't his new friend's real name. 'I hope you will sleep well, and I shall wake you at seven o'clock tomorrow morning.'

The bed proved as comfortable as it looked, the house was quiet, and Spiky easily forgot about the Brain Sharpeners and was sound asleep inside two minutes. He awoke to Helmut shaking him by the shoulder. Helmut was already dressed; his skin glowed from the effects of a good wash, and not a hair of his head was out of place.

'Seven o'clock, Simon. The bathroom is ready for use.'

'Thanks,' said Simon, pulling the duvet further over his head.

'I have already studied for one hour,' said Helmut, annoyed by Spiky's slow response.

Spiky made some reply from beneath the duvet which Helmut could not hear clearly, which was just as well. Left to himself, Spiky decided he had better not be late for breakfast, in case the matter should be reported to Mr Browser or Mrs Somervil. He couldn't altogether trust a boy who had done an hour's study by seven o'clock in the morning.

At breakfast it was somehow comforting to see Frau Schneider slopping about in a dressing-gown and bedroom slippers, yawning and obviously complaining as her husband stood in her way at the kitchen stove. Breakfast for the Schneiders was usually rolls and butter and cold meats, but Herr Schneider triumphantly brought Spiky a plate with something fried on it.

'Here, Simon, I make you an English breakfast—bacon and an egg.'

The egg was acceptable, and Spiky ate the 'bacon' out of gratitude, though it tasted quite different from the bacon he ate at home.

'We call it *Schinken*,' explained Helmut. Frau Schneider watched Spiky suspiciously, perhaps afraid that she might be expected to cook something like this every morning while Spiky was there. For her the effort of putting out the rolls and butter and making the coffee was quite enough at that time of day.

'Today I will take you to school in my car,' announced Herr Schneider cheerfully. 'Simon, you can sit in the front and keep a good watch for criminals—but there aren't many in Bad Unterfeld.'

Driving to school in a police car was an enjoyable experience for Spiky. People waved and greeted Herr Schneider as he passed them, and it seemed that the life of a policeman in Bad Unterfeld was not an unhappy one. The journey was over all too quickly, and they drew up in front of the Franz Schubert School.

'Thanks very much!' said Spiky gratefully as he

stepped out of the car.

'A pleasure, Simon,' replied the policeman.

'Call me Spiky,' said Spiky, and the policeman laughed.

'Okay, Spiky! It's a good name. It suits your hair. Helmut, do not work too hard today. Have a good time, Spiky.'

As the car moved away, Spiky wished that the policeman's son was as cheerful as his father, who clearly himself could not completely understand Helmut's sudden earnest love of working. He went with Helmut into the playground behind the school, where groups of children were standing about. The visitors were gradually edging towards each other, anxious to share experiences.

'I'm in a smashing house,' said Anna. 'It's all pot plants, and it's like a greenhouse inside. Astrid's mum is ever so nice—but Astrid spent most of the time doing homework. They must be given a huge amount!'

'Mine was up at six working,' said Spiky. 'But his mum and dad are all right.'

'My one is an expert on everything, but especially science,' said Selwyn. 'His parents think he's wonderful, and told me he's going to be a professor when he grows up.'

'Not another one!' said Spiky. The rest were surprised that Selwyn, the most studious of them all, was talking as though he had been left far behind.

'Can it be that they're all clever here?' asked Anna. 'I know the water's supposed to be special, but I'm beginning to wish I hadn't come, I feel so ignorant—'

'Mine's called Siegfried,' said Michael Fairlie, 'and his parents told me he's changed completely in the past three weeks. He used to be mad on football and gymnastics, but now he can't keep his head out of books on mathematics. It reminds me of something—of when you lot were a bit like that.'

He paused, and looked puzzled, as though there was something else to add which he just couldn't remember.

'You mean,' said Anna, recalling her dream, 'that it reminds you of when the Brain Sharpeners tried to grab us. There's something odd happening here; Mike said Siegfried has changed suddenly, Selwyn said Sebastian is too clever for words, Astrid has time for nothing but homework, and Spiky's friend's parents can't understand what's become of their son. I reckon they're all in danger, and it's up to us to make certain. You can't tell me it's normal for everybody in a class to be swots, whatever country one's in!'

'It surely can't be the Brain Sharpeners,' muttered Michael, his mind disturbed by memories.

'Watch out for anything suspicious, that's all I say,' warned Anna as they filed into school.

The visitors were received into Fräulein Schmidt's

classroom, where after calling the register she dealt with arrangements for the day, and then asked the Chivvy Chase children if there were any difficulties which they wanted to raise. Problems there appeared to be none; if any of the visitors couldn't control the duvets or digest the food, they were too polite to mention it; and nobody was going to admit that the hosts were far too clever for comfort.

At this point Herr Weissmann appeared and took over the meeting.

'Any complaints?' he asked Mr Browser, who was pleased to report none.

'Very good,' said the Headmaster. 'It is nice for the Franz Schubert children and the Chivvy Chase children to be together, but unfortunately that cannot always be so, as Class S has very much work to do. I have arranged that this morning the class will be taken by me, and Fräulein Schmidt will conduct the English children through the town, showing them the town hall, the park in which the Bad Unterfeld spring water flows, the art gallery and the statue of Goethe. When you return, you will be able to go home with the children of Class S. I hope you will like our town, and that the weather will be fine for you all to visit the swimming pool this afternoon.'

'That's better! The swimming pool is supposed to be very good,' whispered Michael. 'Siegfried told me it has artificial waves and you can swim from a warm pool into a cooler one, if you want to.'

'Do you think our friends are going to be given time to go swimming?' put in Anna. 'That man can't wait to start them working, and I bet he sets them hours of homework. They'll have to stay up late to make up for it if they're allowed to go swimming as well.'

'Please follow me,' said Fräulein Schmidt, and Mr Caracco led out behind her. As the English children followed, Herr Weissmann had no more time for them; he was already writing some mathematical signs on the blackboard in spidery writing.

'I'm sure I'm right, Spiky,' whispered Anna earnestly as they walked out of the main doors. 'Follow that man, and he'll lead you to the Brain Sharpeners. He's in their power, and if something isn't done, all of Class S will be completely under their control too, and soon they'll vanish just as completely as the children of Hamelin did in the story of the Pied Piper.'

'Form into twos,' ordered Mr Browser, who was at the back of the line. 'And if you talk, do so quietly, please. We want to show a good example to the people of Bad Unterfeld.'

Anna paired up with Alison, and Spiky with Michael, and neither pair had any desire to talk too loudly. Indeed, they had so much on their minds that for a while they didn't talk at all.

Back at the Franz Schubert School Class S had their heads down and were taking notes as fast as Herr

Weissmann could write them on the board; what they were learning was material usually intended for seventeen-year-olds.

While he was proudly working and hoping to turn the Franz Schubert School into the most famous one in all Germany, the Brain Sharpeners out in space were preparing for their next visit to Earth, and working out when and how they would transport Class S into space and use them for their own purposes.

3

Deep in the Forest

The morning tour of Bad Unterfeld was much more enjoyable than Spiky and the rest had expected, mainly because the town hall turned out to have a restaurant in its cellar, in which the guests were treated to two glasses of delightfully cool fruit juice at the expense of the mayor and corporation of Bad Unterfeld.

In spite of the language difficulties, Fräulein Schmidt and Mr Caracco, and to a lesser extend Mr Browser, all seemed to be getting on like a house on fire, and the rest of the party mostly chattered away happily, pleased to be surrounded by the familiar sounds of their own tongue. This gave Spiky, Anna, Michael and Selwyn, who were sitting at a table on their own, the chance to have a much more serious conversation.

'I don't think that Fräulein Schmidt wanted the Headmaster to take her class this morning,' said Anna. 'She looked at them in a funny way, as though they were being taken away from her.'

'If the Brain Sharpeners are after them, then she's right,' said Michael. 'You should have seen what you lot were like when you were in their power. You were unbearably clever, Spiky!'

'All right, all right—I'm not now, am I?' replied Spiky. 'But I reckon I'm going to find Helmut pretty unbearable. He's not like his father at all.'

'It's the same with them all, from what I've heard,' said Michael. 'And either the parents can't understand what's happened and are just confused, or else they're stupidly proud of their clever children. It's all coming clear to me—the Brain Sharpeners are using this Herr Weissmann like they tried to use Mr Browser. The point is, what are we going to do?'

'At least there's four of us who are aware of what's going on,' said Anna. 'This Fräulein Schmidt doesn't seem to be part of it all, so couldn't we tell her?'

They looked up, to see Fräulein Schmidt managing to laugh at a joke of Mr Caracco's which Mr Browser evidently didn't find all that funny.

'She's nice, but she's too young for a teacher,' said Spiky. 'She couldn't stand up against Herr Weissmann even if she did want to help us. I bet she can't understand what her own class are learning about, and she's scared stiff.'

'How about Browser?' asked Selwyn.

'Maybe later on,' said Spiky. 'But at the moment he's so concerned that we behave ourselves that I don't suppose he'd want to believe anything like that about some foreign kids—not until we have proof.'

'Then it's up to us to find proof,' said Michael, 'but how do we do it?'

'We have to follow the movements of the Headmaster,' suggested Selwyn. 'He must be in touch with the Brain Sharpeners, and sooner or later he'll be taking Class S for what he thinks will be another sharpening—'

'But more likely to be transported to a different space system as slaves,' put in Michael.

'We don't know how advanced they are,' said Spiky. 'All we can do is our best. First we keep our eyes on Herr Weissmann, then.'

'Agreed,' said Anna.

'Has he a car?' asked Michael.

'An important point,' declared Selwyn. 'The Brain Sharpeners won't want to let any other people know about them, so they probably won't come anywhere near the school. A fog would be highly suspicious at this time of year.'

'He couldn't take a whole class to them in a car,' declared Michael. 'But here comes Mr Browser. Let's ask him.'

Mr Browser, perhaps a little weary of listening to Mrs Somervil on the history of Bad Unterfeld—Mr Caracco and Fräulein Schmidt were busy trying to sort out their own language difficulties—stood up and wandered round to each table in turn to ask how his pupils were enjoying life. Anna was the first to speak when he came to her table.

'This is the best orange juice I've ever had, Mr

44

Browser,' she said.

'Good,' said Mr Browser. 'And how are things going with all of you?'

'Fine,' replied Spiky. 'I'm looking forward to swimming this afternoon—I hear the pool is great.'

'I think I shall even have a swim myself,' said Mr Browser. 'Are you all settling down well?'

'No trouble, Mr Browser,' said Michael. 'I'm not homesick yet. But they're all so clever, that's the only snag. And they spend all their spare time working. It's a bit like the time—'

'They're very thorough here,' cut in Mr Browser, as if he didn't want to hear any more. 'They probably seem cleverer to you than they really are, because you don't understand the language.'

'Mr Weissmann looks very thorough,' risked Spiky. 'Does he have a car, Mr Browser?'

'No, I don't think he does,' said Mr Browser, surprised. 'Why do you ask?'

'This place is very small, and hidden away in the woods, so I don't suppose one has to have one,' observed Spiky.

'He has a bicycle, I believe,' said Mr Browser. 'But he enjoys walking, he tells me. As a matter of fact, he mentioned that he's going for a walk in the woods this afternoon.'

This remark was greeted with silence.

'Well, drink up your fruit juice,' said Mr Browser,

45

moving on. 'We shall soon be on our way to the art gallery. Please keep your opinions about the pictures to yourself, Simon. They're thought a great deal of here.'

'Bet they're as good as Spiky's own works,' joked Michael, and Mr Browser walked away, smiling. As soon as he was at the next table and out of hearing range, Anna leant across the table.

'There you are—he's going into the woods on his own, and I bet he'll contact the Brain Sharpeners while he's there!'

'Maybe—but we can't do anything about it,' said Selwyn.

'We could follow him,' said Spiky.

'Don't forget, we're supposed to be swimming this afternoon,' Michael reminded him. 'We can't very well refuse to go on the very first afternoon we're here.'

'Maybe we'll have to wait until he arranges for the whole class to go somewhere with him,' admitted Spiky.

'And maybe that'll be too late,' said Anna.

They finished their drinks, and the party moved on to the next stage of its tour, the visit to the art gallery. Apart from a few interesting items about the witches who used to live in Bad Unterfeld, the gallery was not found to be an exciting stop, and Spiky had to use all the reserves of politeness he had to avoid making a nuisance of himself. They arrived back at the Franz

Schubert School hungry and a little tired, and Mrs Somervil did her best to enliven them with a description of the afternoon ahead at the swimming pool.

'You will come to the pool with your German friends at three o'clock,' she told them, 'and after an hour in the water you will all be given a drink and a cake at the café, the money provided for very kindly by Herr Weissmann.'

'He wants us out of the way,' said Anna.

Spiky returned home for lunch with Helmut, who was very pleased with the amount he had learned that morning.

'In the time that Herr Weissmann has taught me, I have learned more quickly then I have ever done before,' he told Spiky.

'Are you sure that's all he's doing?' asked Spiky, and received a look of surprise from Helmut. 'I mean,' added Spiky hastily, 'has Herr Weissmann taken you anywhere in order to help you to learn more quickly?'

Helmut looked blank.

'Herr Weissmann never has time to take us anywhere. Only one time, to the woods to look at the different trees,' he replied. 'We must hurry home to eat now, or I shall not have time to do some of my homework before we go swimming.'

Poor Helmut, thought Spiky, he doesn't even know what's happening to him. He obliged his friend by running with him most of the way to his home, where

48

Frau Schneider had managed to prepare a kind of stew which Spiky was hungry enough to enjoy. The strawberries which followed were delightful, and then Frau Schneider prepared them a drink of coffee and retired with hers for a rest. Helmut insisted on doing some homework, and Spiky occupied himself by writing a few postcards home, having bought some views of Bad Unterfeld that morning. When he had completed them he sat and felt a little sorry for himself, alone in a foreign land and with a new friend who preferred to give his time to something called the Pythagoras Theory rather than to Spiky.

Soon enough, however, Helmut appeared with swimming trunks and a towel, and urged Spiky to fetch his. It was hot that afternoon in sleepy Bad Unterfeld, and Spiky was looking forward to his swim. The party gathered outside the pool, and Spiky noted that Mr Browser and Mrs Somervil were there, but Fräulein Schmidt and Mr Caracco were missing. To his surprise, and that of Anna and Michael, Herr Weissmann appeared as well.

'So much for his walk in the woods,' said Spiky.

'He could still go,' said Anna. 'He hasn't brought any swimming things.'

Soon the party had been under the showers and all were enjoying themselves in the clear water of the pool, which they had to admit was worthy of the praise Mrs Somervil had given it. She and Mr Browser were in

the water too, Mr Browser floating on his back and
giving an imitation of a sea lion, while Inga's mother
energetically showed off her elegant butterfly swimming style. Herr Weissmann stood at the edge of the
pool, smiling down on them and waiting rather
impatiently for Mr Browser to stand on his feet again.

'Enjoy yourselves,' he said when at last this happened. 'I wish you all a most happy afternoon. Goodbye!' He waved, then turned and made to go—but
Mrs Somervil called him across and started to talk to
him about some detail of the day's programme

for tomorrow.

With a few swift strokes Anna was at Spiky's side, treading water. 'He's going,' she said. 'Why don't we follow him?'

'He'd be gone before—'

'No he won't! He's talking to Inga's mum. Quick, Spiky—into the shower and change. The rest won't notice.'

They swam to the side and climbed out of the pool. Mr Browser was floating again, and Inga's mother was still busily in conversation with Herr Weissmann.

'Hurry, Spiky—but we must try not to attract the attention of the pool people,' said Anna.

Drying himself and dressing hadn't been such a problem for Spiky since he was four years old. His shirt sleeves stuck to his arms, his socks had an argument with his feet and his shoelaces seemed determined not to tie into knots. In a quicker time than he imagined he passed out of the exit gate and saw Anna coming from her cubicle. Together they ran to the road and looked up and down it. The road to the left curved very quickly, so that you couldn't see far along it; in the other direction it led to the centre of the town. There was no sign of Herr Weissmann in either direction.

'He could have had time to go to the left,' said Spiky, 'and that way must lead more quickly to the woods. Let's run until we can see round the bend.'

They ran until the curve began, and came to a stop behind the trunk of a large lime tree. Spiky peered round it and up the road.

'He's there!' he said. 'Going up the hill.'

Anna looked too, and saw Herr Weissmann striding out up a slope which led to the end of the road and the beginning of a path into the woods. They started running again, this time at a steady trot, sensing the difficulty which all pursuers have; too close, and you may be seen, too far off and you may lose sight of your quarry.

'Slow down a bit,' ordered Spiky.

'Suppose he sees us?' asked Anna.

'I don't think he will,' replied Spiky. 'He's walking in such a determined way that he probably won't turn round at all until he comes near to the meeting place—if there is one. If he does see us, we'll just have to say we don't like swimming.'

At the entrance to the path there was a sign showing an adult and child, to show that the path was an official one on which people could walk for pleasure. They were thankful that the ground was soft with old pine needles and the remains of last autumn's leaves, so that their footsteps made scarcely any sound at all. Herr Weissmann was way ahead, striding faster than ever.

'There are two people coming towards him,' whispered Anna. 'Let's wait and see what happens.'

'Nothing, I suppose,' said Spiky, but he was soon glad he had stopped. In the distance they could hear the man and woman greeting Herr Weissmann as they passed him.

'*Guten Tag*,' said the man, raising a walking stick in greeting.

'*Guten Tag*,' replied Herr Weissmann.

'Get off the path,' said Spiky. 'If they greet us as well, Herr Weissmann will know someone's behind him, and he might look round.'

They darted off the path into the trees—and instantly Anna felt a little afraid. You only had to move about three trees deep into that wood and you entered a world of darkness, as though the wood were warning you that it was not just a wood, but part of the ancient Teutoburger Forest, a world of its own.

Spiky and Anna held their breath while the hikers, a middle-aged couple, walked earnestly by. The veins on the hikers' legs stood out as if in protest, and perspiration had gathered on their foreheads. Soon they were gone, and Anna and Spiky took to the path again.

'We'd better move faster,' said Spiky. 'He's out of sight, and there might be a junction of paths ahead.'

They soon had Herr Weissmann in view again, and although they kept to the edge of the path, ready to spring out of sight, there was little need to worry. Herr Weissmann took a look at his watch, and then began

53

to run. Spiky looked at his own watch.

'Nearly half past three,' he said. 'I bet he has to be at the chosen place by then. Keep an eye open for anything odd above us, Anna, while I watch him.'

'He's left the path!' whispered Anna. 'Now we might lose him!'

'Run full out!' Spiky ordered her. 'We just can't afford to lose him now!'

They sped along the path, Spiky keeping his eye on the point at which the Headmaster had disappeared. When they arrived there, at first it seemed that Herr Weissmann had simply walked into the thick of the woods.

'We've lost him!' said Anna sadly. 'It would be hopeless to try and find him in that blackness.'

Spiky stood between two trees and studied the ground ahead of them.

'There is a way,' he said, standing up straight. 'Some grass has been flattened between the trees. That's the way he's gone—are you coming?'

Anna thought for a moment of saying no, but then that pride which leads girls to want to show that they can do anything boys can do—and better, came to the fore.

'Of course I am.' But she was grateful that Spiky led the way.

The Teutoburger Forest has always been dark and mysterious, and the bits that remained around Bad

Unterfeld were no different. 'We challenge you to come out of the sunlight and into our world,' the tree trunks seemed to be saying. 'We'll show you that our world is as real as yours.'

Spiky set off confidently enough, but after he had passed a few trees he slowed down. Did the narrow path go straight ahead, or had Herr Weissmann turned to one side? He wished he had a torch, so that he could see the blades of grass—if there were any.

'I'm going straight on,' he told Anna. 'If we go straight, at least we've a hope of finding our way back by turning round and heading in the opposite direction. The path may not go anywhere, but I dare not turn to one side.'

'Keep going,' agreed Anna. 'But not too far.'

She looked behind her, and there was only a faint glimmer of light to show where the path was. The trees were nearly all upright pines, standing like soldiers ready for inspection, and the forest was silent, as though no animals wanted to brave the darkness.

'Can you see anything?' asked Anna.

'Nothing,' replied Spiky.

'Then let's turn back. I'm afraid we'll be lost,' admitted Anna.

'I'm going past two more trees,' said Spiky—and when he had done so he stopped.

'No good?' asked Anna.

'Listen,' said Spiky.

'It's the wind,' said Anna doubtfully as she listened to a whirring sound which came from somewhere ahead of them.

'It could be,' agreed Spiky. 'Or it could be the Brain Sharpeners.'

The power of the wind increased until it became a roar, yet there was no sign of movement among the trees.

'It's not far away,' said Spiky. 'I'm going on a little. Stay here!'

'Not too far, Spiky!'

'I can see light,' whispered Spiky. 'Come on—the wood's only thin after all. I can see some water ahead. Look, Anna!'

They stepped to the edge of the trees, and down below them was a pond. On its bank stood a large hut, intended as a shelter, with one side open. Herr Weissmann was sitting on a bench at the back of the shelter, waiting. The sound of the wind could be heard strengthening above them, and suddenly a kind of tornado-shaped cloud came down, hovered over the pond and then moved towards the bank, where it finally settled.

'They've come!' said Spiky, moving back to make sure that he was completely hidden from view. 'Clever of them—to come inside a sort of tornado. Look what's happening!'

Herr Weissmann stood up, walked towards the

tornado-shaped cloud—and disappeared into it. After a few seconds the cloud rose up, the wind roared, and Herr Weissmann was gone.

'It is them!' cried Anna, white-faced. 'Let's go back, Spiky. I'm afraid.'

'So am I,' said Spiky. 'The question is, has he gone for good?'

'They won't want him alone, Spiky. It's children they're after. They'll probably tell him when they want to collect Class S. And if we're around, they'll take us too!'

'They won't want us,' argued Spiky. 'They haven't sharpened our brains.'

'But if we know too much—'

'The Brain Sharpeners mustn't find out we're here,' said Spiky. 'We'd better keep well away from this point so that when the Headmaster returns, if he does, he won't suspect that we know anything.'

'Suppose he's told them our party from Chivvy Chase is in Bad Unterfeld?'

'I doubt if he will,' said Spiky. 'He'll be so occupied with making his own children clever, that he'll not think about us. And as long as he thinks we suspect nothing, he won't worry. If he does tell them, the chances are they'll just act more quickly to kidnap Class S. They must know by now that they're succeeding in sharpening their brains—those kids are just loving it! We'll have to warn everyone we can of the danger, even if we are laughed at—let's get back to the swimming pool as quickly as we can!'

'About turn,' said Anna. 'Walk in a straight line behind me.'

They didn't keep quite straight, and Anna's heart beat faster as she wondered whether they had managed to lose themselves even in that narrow strip of forest. But suddenly the sun's rays showed where the path was, and they stepped out from the trees and started to run back the same way that they had come.

'Who's going to believe us?' panted Anna.

'You can't be sure of the adults, but surely plenty of Class 8 will,' said Spiky. 'Michael and Selwyn for sure—we'll have to start on them—'

'Two people coming!' Anna warned him.

'Never mind that,' said Spiky. 'Why—it's Mr Caracco and that Fräulein Schmidt, Class S's teacher!'

The two teachers were walking along arm in arm, and were talking together as if they'd known one another for years, instead of only one and a half days.

'Shall we tell them?' asked Anna.

'Why not—there'll be nothing lost,' said Spiky, and the pair slowed up as they came face to face with the teachers.

Mr Caracco didn't seem at all pleased to see them, and Fräulein Schmidt looked most surprised, and quickly took her arm away from Mr Caracco's.

'What are you two doing here?' demanded Mr Caracco. 'Shouldn't you be swimming?'

'We were,' said Anna. 'But something happened.'

'What happened?'

'We saw the Headmaster leave the pool, and we followed him,' said Spiky, and hurried to explain himself as Mr Caracco started to ask him why. 'We thought that he was going to meet some—some creatures who are trying to take over Class S.'

Fräulein Schmidt was struggling to understand what he was talking about, and Mr Caracco, who had joined Chivvy Chase School after the first arrival of the Brain Sharpeners, looked stern.

'You're talking in riddles, Simon,' he said. 'Are you trying to find an excuse for being where you shouldn't be?'

'No, no, Mr Caracco! Class S is in real danger—their brains are being sharpened by the Brain Sharpeners, who will take them off to another planet if they're not stopped. Ask Mr Browser, Mr Caracco. He knows about them. And we've just seen their Headmaster disappear into a sort of cloud—they've taken him to give him their latest instructions. It's true, Mr Caracco. You only have to see the work these children are doing and you'll realise it's not natural. My friend Helmut, he's working all hours of the day, and I can't understand what he's on about!'

'Probably because it's in German—'

'No—I mean the maths,' Spiky interrupted him, but Mr Caracco was not to be convinced.

'Simon—and you too, Anna—you had better report back to the swimming pool at once. I just don't understand what you're talking about.'

'He disappeared, Mr Caracco, he did, honestly.'

'I shall expect to see you with the others when I return,' insisted Mr Caracco. 'Now go!'

There was no denying him, but as he turned to go Spiky had one last try to make him listen.

'Please tell Mr Browser about the Brain Sharpeners,' he begged. 'They're trying again, and they've taken the Headmaster over, I'm certain.'

'All right, Simon, hurry along now,' replied Mr Caracco, speaking as though Spiky were a small child not to be taken seriously.

Anna and Spiky could only obey and trot on down the path.

'You see the way people act when we tell them what's happened,' said Spiky. 'They just won't believe us. I can't see how we're ever going to stop the Brain Sharpeners.'

The conversation which followed between Mr Caracco and Fräulein Schmidt would have surprised him if he had heard it.

'That boy said—the brains of my class have been interfered with?' she asked.

'That's right,' replied Mr Caracco. 'He was making

61

up some tale, I suppose, to excuse himself for being where he shouldn't have been.'

'But it is strange—for some time it is true that the children have changed. They are all working so hard now, and becoming so clever. Yes, they are so clever that I cannot myself understand all that they are learning. It is like that since Herr Weissmann has begun to teach them himself, before three weeks. It is strange, how he can do it. He teaches them for several lessons each day now—before that he did not teach much at all.'

'It is odd,' agreed Mr Caracco without giving the matter much thought. 'But children never surprise me.' (This he had heard Mr Browser saying.)

'If we are going to have a cup of coffee,' said Fräulein Schmidt, 'we had better hurry up. I know an excellent café in the town where nice cream cakes are baked.'

They linked arms again and strolled slowly towards the town.

Five minutes later they were overtaken by a single man going the same way. Mr Caracco stood to one side to allow him to pass. Suddenly Fräulein Schmidt spoke in German, and Mr Caracco saw that the person she was greeting was Herr Weissmann. There was perspiration on the Headmaster's forehead, and his blue eyes shone with anxiety as he saw who they were.

'Herr Caracco! It is a surprise to see you!' he said, and then he spoke quickly in German to Fräulein Schmidt again. 'I must go,' he said in farewell to Mr Caracco. 'There is much for me to do!'

He was almost running as he hastened away from them, and Fräulein Schmidt watched him with surprised eyes.

'You know,' she said to Mr Caracco, 'there is indeed something strange about Herr Weissmann lately. He really is a most nice man, and does not require too much work to be done. He used to say if we are happy we will do better. But now, since three weeks, all he wants is work and more work. He even says he will teach my class *Germanistik*, and that is something for the university students! Oh dear, Mr Caracco, I am a fish in deep water, I think you say.'

She looked up at him with such a troubled expression that he hadn't the heart to tell her that she meant to compare herself to a fish out of water.

'Let's have our cups of coffee,' he said, and they walked on in troubled silence.

4

A Suitable Subject for Sharpening

When they arrived back at the pool Spiky and Anna were greeted by a number of highly curious children, both English and German.

'Where have you gone?' asked Helmut of Spiky as they sat down at a table in the swimming pool restaurant, where the children were now enjoying refreshments.

'I will bring you a piece of cake, Anna,' said Astrid. 'Which do you like, strawberry or apple cake? We were afraid you had sunk to the bottom of the pool.'

'Strawberry, please,' said Anna. 'I'm sorry you were worried—we were tired of swimming and went for a walk.'

'It has worried your teacher and Frau Somervil very much,' said Helmut critically. 'It would be much better if you told us before you leave—'

'I'm very sorry,' said Spiky as Selwyn and Michael came to join them, closely followed by Mr Browser and Mrs Somervil. Spiky made a quick sign to Anna that the truth could not yet be told, and they had to sit there and take the blame for their unreasonable behaviour.

'I cannot understand you at all!' declared Inga's

64

mother. 'Such a beautiful swimming pool, and you are both keen swimmers, and yet you run off like that! You do not deserve to come on such a visit! I shall inform Mr Sage as soon as the party arrives home!'

Mr Browser was a little less excited about it, but nevertheless was not pleased.

'Please see that nothing of this kind happens again!' he warned them. 'What an example to set to your German friends! You are not infants, but running away like that is infant behaviour. You have let me down, both of you!'

Anna was ready to cry, and Spiky was bursting to tell him the truth, but he sensed that while Helmut, Astrid and Mrs Somervil were within hearing distance, it was better to sit and suffer. The moment to talk did not come until they were all moving out of the restaurant.

'Mr Browser—may we speak to you alone? We couldn't talk in front of the others.'

'What do you mean?' demanded Mr Browser, looking down severely at Spiky. But he obligingly stepped to one side so that no one else could hear them.

'We had a reason for going, Mr Browser. We followed the Headmaster, and he was taken up by the Brain Sharpeners. They're back, Mr Browser, and they have him and Class S in their power. That's why the children are all so clever!'

Mr Browser stared hard and long at both of them, so that they felt like mindless worms.

'Simon,' he said, 'sometimes I think the hot sun over here or the change of food have gone to your head. You're talking utter nonsense, boy!'

'It isn't nonsense,' pleaded Anna. 'We saw him disappear, and we can show you where it happened. Class S are in big danger, Mr Browser!'

'I think,' said Mr Browser, 'that you'd better go home with your friends and forget all about this.

You're letting the fact that these children are so much more clever go to your heads. Maybe they just work harder than you do!'

'Come, Simon,' called out Helmut. 'I must quickly go home. I have much work to do!'

'There you are!' said Spiky. 'Work is all he thinks about. It isn't much of a holiday for us, because they're all as bad.'

'I wouldn't call working bad, Simon,' said Mr Browser.

'Astrid's the same, Mr Browser,' began Anna, but Inga's mother arrived to hurry Mr Browser on his way.

'If he won't believe us, who will?' said Spiky dejectedly. 'Either he can't remember the Brain Sharpeners, or else he doesn't want to remember them. Maybe he's afraid of upsetting Herr Weissmann.'

'All I know is, I'm keeping well away from that pond in the woods,' declared Anna. 'See you in the morning, Spiky. Don't work too hard.'

She walked away with Astrid, and Helmut came to meet Spiky, who had little to say to him as they walked towards his house at a brisk pace. Once arrived there, Helmut politely switched on the television set in order to occupy Spiky, and then went into his bedroom to work on his homework. German television, like English, can be boring at times, and for Spiky there was the additional difficulty that he couldn't understand what the people were talking

67

about. His attention wandered, but after his unusual day he was fairly content to sit comfortably in a chair—though his mind was much disturbed.

There was no relief for him until Herr Schneider came home and Frau Schneider called on them to eat the dinner she had prepared. Spiky was hungry enough to enjoy it, but he was dismayed to see Helmut return to his work immediately afterwards. Frau Schneider was busy clearing up, and the policeman joined Spiky in front of the television. A man was talking, and what he was saying appeared to interest the policeman no more than it did Spiky. Suddenly he walked across and switched the set off, and then looked at Spiky with some sympathy.

'Helmut—very busy,' said Herr Schneider. 'He is not ever like this.'

'Not always?' suggested Spiky.

'Yes—not always, I mean. He plays games like football—and cards. Life is not all work for him, but now all is changed.'

Spiky nodded agreement—and then had a sudden thought. This policeman seemed a sensible man; he was clearly doubtful about his son's behaviour, and maybe he would listen to Spiky's story, if only he could be made to understand it. Spiky spoke slowly and clearly.

'What kind of man is Herr Weissmann, the Headmaster? Do you like him?'

'Yes,' replied the policeman. 'A very good man, the children all like him.'

'But he is like Helmut now,' went on Spiky. 'He only wants to work, and make the children cleverer than any other children.'

'Yes, he is teaching very hard.'

'He is bringing Helmut and all the children into danger,' said Spiky. 'He is being controlled—he is not himself.'

'He is not himself?' repeated the policeman. 'Who is he, then?'

'Mr Schneider,' said Spiky in a sudden burst of desperation, 'your son is in great trouble—great danger. So are all his friends. All his *Kamaraden*—all in much danger!'

Spiky realised to the full that however much you may want another person to understand, all the will in the world cannot quickly overcome the language problem. Fortunately, though, the expression on Spiky's face told the policeman as much as his words could manage.

'Danger? All his friends have danger?' he said. 'I bring Helmut—he will understand.'

'Oh no!' objected Spiky, but the policeman was not to be stopped from calling his son. Helmut came in, annoyed to have been interrupted in his work. His father was talking to him energetically in German, and Helmut's answer seemed to Spiky to express

69

his irritation.

'Simon, I do not understand my father,' he said. 'He talks of danger—what is it about?'

Spiky was unwilling to say much, for he feared that if the Brain Sharpeners were in charge of Helmut, they would soon find out if Helmut's thoughts revealed that their plans were being suspected by other people.

'Helmut, you have been to the woods with Class S, haven't you?'

'Yes,' replied Helmut. 'It was a walk with Herr Weissmann to look at a pond, that is all.'

'Are you sure that is all? Didn't something else happen?'

'Something else? Astrid nearly fell in the water, that is all.'

'Nothing else? Didn't something come down from the sky, and didn't Herr Weissmann lead you all into this thing—'

'Thing? Sky? You are speaking nonsense,' declared Helmut, and turned in disgust to talk with his father in German. All the time Helmut was edging towards the door, keen to return to his work, and it looked to Spiky as though his father was suggesting that he ought to be spending more time with Spiky. Helmut had his hand on the door, when the conversation was interrupted by the buzzing of the front door bell. Herr Schneider went to answer it, and Helmut took the opportunity to slip away to his studies.

70

A moment later Spiky heard a familiar voice talking to Herr Schneider in German, and Inga's mother, Mrs Somervil, entered the room. Having arranged the Chivvy Chase School visit, she was most anxious that it should be successful, and the behaviour of Spiky and Anna that afternoon had upset her very much. She gave Spiky one of her nervous, intense looks, as if daring him to step out of line again.

'Well, Simon,' she said, 'I have come to make sure that you are getting on all right here. That is so, isn't it? You have no grumbles, I suppose? I think not. Mr and Mrs Schneider will be looking after you, I am sure.'

All the time she was speaking she was looking at Spiky as if trying to work out why he should have gone off in secret in the woods that afternoon.

'They are very good to me,' said Spiky, 'but Helmut is always working, so I don't see very much of him.'

'Yes, the children of Class S are very hard workers,' said Mrs Somervil approvingly. 'They set a good example to you all.'

'Do they!' muttered Spiky—and Inge Somervil spoke again in German with Herr Schneider. With some difficulty the policeman appeared to be trying to make her listen. She stared hard at Spiky, and at last could remain silent no longer.

'Whatever is all this nonsense you have been telling Herr Schneider?' she demanded. 'And why did you go

71

off to the woods this afternoon, instead of swimming with the rest?'

'It wasn't nonsense!' burst out Spiky. 'And if your daughter Inga had been in the class all this year, she could have told you why it's not nonsense. The Brain Sharpeners are back, and they've taken control of Helmut and his class, and the Headmaster. That's why Helmut is working so hard. He's not usually like that—ask his dad!'

'I don't see anything wrong in working hard,' said Inga's mother. 'Some of you children in Class 8 would do well to follow Helmut's example.'

'You'll soon find out what's wrong when the Brain Sharpeners make off with all of them,' insisted Spiky. 'They'll take them up into space and use them as slaves on one of their planets, and then they'll probably return for more children.'

'What nonsense! You can't expect me to believe that—'

'No, I don't,' said Spiky. 'But Anna and I followed the Headmaster this afternoon, and we saw him taken up by the Brain Sharpeners. He's their agent now, Mrs Somervil, I'm sure of it.'

Helmut's father put a question in German to Mrs Somervil, who answered energetically, raising her arms in the air to show her despair at Spiky's failure to talk sense. Then Herr Schneider talked, and although Spiky couldn't understand a word, it was easy for him

72

to grasp that Helmut's father was much more kindly disposed towards him than was Mrs Somervil. She kept on shrugging her shoulders and shaking her head, but after a while she turned to Spiky.

'Herr Schneider is very worried about you, Simon,' she began. 'He thinks you are lonely, perhaps because Helmut is working so much, and that is why you are making up such tales. He would like to take you out in his car to make a change for you.'

'I'm not making up tales,' grumbled Spiky, and to his surprise the policeman put his hand on his shoulder.

'You come—to the wood,' he said. 'I will see where Herr Weissmann did go.'

'Yes, of course I'll show you,' said Spiky, greatly relieved to find that someone at least was treating him as sane.

To his further surprise, Herr Schneider appeared to be insisting that Inga's mother came with them. He said goodbye to his wife, and the three of them set off in his private car towards the woods. He parked the car at the end of the road where the path to the woods began, and then urged Spiky to lead the way. Inga's mother looked very fed up, perhaps because she had other children to visit that evening, and also because the policeman had taken charge of the situation, which didn't suit her.

The sun was going down, and the shadows on the

path were merging into one big shadow. The police-man and Mrs Somervil were talking together in German, and as Spiky drew nearer to the point where he and Anna had left the path he became uneasy, not so much at the prospect of turning off into the trees in the near darkness, but at the thought of what might be waiting for them at the edge of the pool.

'This is where we left the path,' he told Mrs Somervil.

'Oh, I know that pond,' she replied. 'I used to go there when I was a child. There's another path a little further on which leads to it. There's no need to scramble through the trees.'

She turned to Herr Schneider and talked with him again in German, pointing to her shoes and stockings. 'You go that way with Herr Schneider,' she then told Spiky. 'I don't want to tear my clothes—it'll be quite dark among the trees. I'll see you in a few minutes—I'm going to take the path.'

She walked away down the track, and Spiky and the policeman took to the woods. Now that he knew the way, Spiky found the distance to the pond much shorter than it had seemed in the afternoon. Soon they were staring down at the pond, Spiky pointing to the place where Herr Weissmann had disappeared into the Brain Sharpeners' craft. The policeman looked at the spot with interest, and signed to Spiky that he wanted to inspect it more closely.

They began to move down the hillside, concentrating on keeping their balance, when Spiky heard that familiar roaring sound. He stopped and grabbed the policeman's arm. Herr Schneider smiled. 'The wind,' he said, pleased that the word for wind is the same in German as in English. 'It is coming strong.'

'No,' replied Spiky. 'It's the Brain Sharpeners. Look!'

The policeman looked puzzled, then disturbed, then amazed as the wind descended in cone shape to the edge of the pond.

'*Ein Wirbelsturm*!' he said, talking to himself. Spiky guessed what he meant.

'It's not a storm—not a tornado,' he said. 'It looks like one, but it's the new way the Brain Sharpeners have disguised their space craft. Look—it's stopping. Come back into the trees, Herr Schneider—perhaps they've come for us!'

Spiky was so excited and anxious that the policeman allowed himself to be pulled back under cover of the trees. The cloud like formation settled down in one position on the bank, and was spinning more and more slowly, until finally the cloud dispersed like steam into the air and a cone-shaped white object remained by the pond.

'A pepperpot!' whispered Spiky, trembling. 'That's the shape they use. They've come back! Let's go, Mr Schneider! They'll take us away—don't let them take

75

me away, please!'

Herr Schneider stood there spellbound, looking from the pepperpot object to Spiky, and then back at it again, so that Spiky began to fear that the policeman was already under the influence of the Brain Sharpeners.

'If you don't go, I shall!' he cried in desperation. 'I won't let them control me—come away, please!'

'Stop!' said the policeman, and pointed to a different part of the bank of the pond. 'Frau Somervil!'

Angry at the delay, Spiky turned to look. Mrs Somervil was walking to the pond, along a path which came out of the woods along level ground.

'Mrs Somervil!' Spiky shouted. 'Stop! Don't let them take you!'

The policeman sensed danger.

'Frau Somervil! *Wir kommen! Warten Sie, bitte!'*

He was giving the same message as Spiky had given, but Inge Somervil was in no mood to listen. Without giving any sign that she knew they had called to her, she walked straight on, and they watched breathlessly as she approached the pepperpot object.

A door opened in its side—and as though she had expected this to happen, Inga's mother walked calmly into the pepperpot. The door closed after her, and the roaring of the wind began again. Soon the white pepperpot seemed to turn grey as it became enveloped in cloud like gas, and soon it was spinning so fast that

only a grey mass could be made out. Gradually it lifted off the ground, then moved swiftly upwards as if sucked up from above.

Suddenly there was nothing left. Mrs Somervil had vanished completely.

'The Brain Sharpeners took her!' said Spiky, and suddenly thought that this was not so surprising; Mrs Somervil was a likely person for them to capture. Quite why he thought this, he couldn't understand. Then he became conscious of the policeman beside him.

'The Brain Sharpeners,' said Herr Schneider. 'How you are right, Simon. What we can do, to save all the others, and Frau Somervil?'

'Mrs Somervil will come back,' Spiky tried to assure him. 'But when she comes—she will be in their power.'

Herr Schneider looked puzzled, and Spiky applied a finger to his head in an effort to explain, without much success. The policeman was on his side, it was clear, but the problem of making him understand the methods and the object of the Brain Sharpeners was too difficult for Spiky.

'We must talk to Mr Browser,' he said. 'He can speak some German, and he knows about the Brain Sharpeners, if only we can make him admit to it.'

'Come, then, to Mr Browser,' said the policeman, still looking back to the spot where Mrs Somervil had disappeared. 'I must speak also with Herr Weissmann about her.'

'No, not with Herr Weissmann!' begged Spiky. 'The Brain Sharpeners already have him in their power. He won't help you at all!'

Herr Schneider shook his head and started to climb back to the path through the trees.

'Brain Sharpeners,' he kept muttering. 'Brain Sharpeners. Where come they from?'

'Outer Space,' said Spiky, and pointed up in the direction of a faint star which had appeared above the path. The policeman looked up at the sky, then at Spiky, and shook his head again.

There had never been a case like this in the history of Bad Unterfeld.

'Think of Helmut,' said Spiky, in case Herr Schneider was beginning to doubt what he had seen. 'We must save him!'

'Yes, poor Helmut,' said his father, and quickened his pace. 'We find Herr Browser now, and perhaps I understand more.'

Spiky was happy to have to run alongside him in order to keep up with him. For it meant that at least one person now realised that something strange was threatening Class S of the Franz Schubert School.

If only Mr Browser would believe it too!

5

Shocks for the Brain Sharpeners

The Brain Sharpeners, dismayed by their several failures to capture the young humans of Chivvy Chase School for their colonisation experiment, were happy to call off their attempt to enslave human beings and search elsewhere in the universe for suitable slaves. They came across the Quadropoles, creatures with four arms and four hands on each arm. The expedition to Earth was withdrawn, and the Quadropoles, who were much less stubborn than the humans, were easily captured and taken to Planet Z13, which the Brain Sharpeners wanted to develop. The brains of the Quadropoles were small, but the Brain Sharpeners believed that they had sharpened them enough for them to be able to do the work required to turn the deserts of Z13 into areas fit for Brain Sharpeners to live in.

Soon reports began to come in from Z13 that the Quadropoles were not performing as well as had been hoped. The sharpening of their brains seemed to have caused the nerves running to their hands to act in different ways, as though each hand received slightly different commands from the others. To put it bluntly, one hand didn't know what the others were doing.

The result was disaster for the buildings that were supposed to be built for their masters. Walls and roofs collapsed, and each building failed to get off the ground. The Quadropoles rushed about in confusion, sometimes getting their own hands twisted together, and sometimes getting themselves entangled with each other. The experiment was an utter failure.

'Get rid of them as quickly as you can!' ordered the Prime Brain Sharpener ruthlessly. 'Throw them out into space, if necessary. The English humans had only two hands, but if only they had been willing, I'm sure they could have worked well for us. Who would have believed that intelligence in the rest of the universe could be so low! And then our only hope, the humans, turned out to be so stubborn!'

Then the Commander of the Earth Expedition saw his chance to come into favour again.

'It was the English children who were so stubborn, Your Primeness,' he said. 'We only tried them. There are other peoples on Earth who may behave different-ly.'

'Such as?' asked the Prime Brain Sharpener coldly.

'I will consult my Chief Earth Researcher,' said the Commander. 'I believe he made some long-distance studies of peoples on Earth, in case our experiment went ahead.'

'Do so,' said the Prime Brain Sharpener. 'Anything would be better than these absurd Quadropoles!'

82

So the Commander had a long visiphone conversation with the Chief Researcher, who presented him with reports on most of the nations of the world.

'With respect, Commander,' concluded the Chief Researcher, 'I would highly recommend your trying out some children from Germany. They are reasonably intelligent by Earth standards, they have a good reputation for working, they are generally strong, and they will no doubt travel well to Planet Z13.'

'Will their brains be up to doing what we require of them?'

'Earth brains are all much the same,' declared the Chief Researcher. 'Claims made on Earth that one nation's children are naturally more gifted than others can be dismissed as nonsense. We have been looking especially at a small town called Bad Unterfeld, which is in the middle of a forest such as you often find on Earth. It would be the ideal place for a quiet brain sharpening experiment. The children's brains would be sharp before anyone would suspect us; we could have them on Planet Z13 before anybody important on Earth started to ask questions. There's nobody very important in Bad Unterfeld, I can assure you, and the Headmaster is just the kind of earnest man to be persuaded that a little brain sharpening would be good for his children.'

So the Commander made a study of the area, agreed that as it was surrounded by woods it would be ideal for the Brain Sharpeners' secret sharpening activities, and the Franz Schubert School was selected, partly because the Brain Sharpeners approved of Herr Weissmann very much. As the experiment progressed, and Helmut and his friends were drawn into the power of the Brain Sharpeners, the Commander was most pleased with the way things were going. He reported to the Prime Brain Sharpener in glowing terms.

'We should have come here in the first place,' he said. 'These children are excellent subjects, ideal for colonising Z13.'

'Are there no awkward children, such as we came up against at Chivvy Chase School?' asked the Prime Brain Sharpener. The Commander groaned.

'Don't remind me of them,' he said. 'No, each one of these children seems well disposed, and I anticipate no trouble at all.'

'Good. Continue as quickly as you can,' ordered the Prime Brain Sharpener. 'Have them sharpened up and transferred to Planet Z13 as soon as possible. If they do well there, we'll arrange to have many more sharpened, and you will be appointed Commander in Chief of Colonisation.'

As a result of this the Commander was so pleased that he sat back and allowed his lesser Brain Sharpeners to do most of the work in keeping an eye on the little victims. It seemed to him that nothing could go wrong, until one day a young Brain Sharpener who had been on Earth watch begged permission to speak to him on the visiphone.

'What is it?' asked the Commander irritably. 'You know I don't wish to be disturbed unless it's a very urgent matter.'

'This could be, Commander,' insisted the young Brain Sharpener. 'Other children have appeared in Bad Unterfeld—about thirty of them. They appear to be on a visit to the Franz Schubert School.'

'Well, no matter,' replied the Commander. 'No doubt they'll go away again. Where do they come from—the next town?'

'No, Commander. That's the curious part of it. They speak English, and they come from—'

The young Sharpener hesitated.

'Yes?' snapped the Commander. 'From?'

'From Chivvy Chase School, Chivvy Chase in England, Commander,' said the Sharpener respectfully.

The Commander flicked off the visiphone for a few seconds so that the young Sharpener couldn't see how pale his cheeks had become and how the brain veins were standing out on his head. There were beads of perspiration on his forehead. He felt his brain cells jangling with shock, but he called on all the mental resources of his kind and switched on again.

'Who is in charge of these children?' he demanded.

'Not that Browser fellow again?'

'He is there,' replied the young Brain Sharpener. 'But the party appears mostly to be in charge of a female human. She is very active, and she speaks both English and German. She talks faster than all the rest, so that it is hard even for a Brain Sharpener to translate all she says. She tells them all what to do, including Herr Weissmann, the Headmaster, and Mr Browser.'

The Commander was feeling as unlucky as a man who has just gambled everything and lost the very roof over his head.

'Michael Fairlie! Spiky Jackson! Anna Cardwell! Not them again!'

He rested his big Brain Sharpener head on his hands.

'Would you like to see them for yourself, Commander?' asked the young Brain Sharpener. 'I'll put you through to Bad Unterfeld.'

They were the last people the Commander wanted to see again—but he had to try and take command. If he were to fail again, there was no knowing what the Prime Brain Sharpener might do.

When he looked through the long-range viewer put at his disposal, his heart sank even lower. There they were, the unmistakable Spiky, Michael, Anna, Selwyn and most of the rest of Class 8, mixing with the brain-sharpened victims of the Franz Schubert

School. There was Mr Browser, drifting about trying to look happy, along with Herr Weissmann and a chubby, fair-haired female as yet unknown to the Commander. He was much impressed by the behaviour of this lady, after spending some time studying her. Not only did she appear to be in a much greater hurry than anyone else, but she also told everyone what to do, including Mr Browser and the Headmaster.

The Commander called a conference with the Brain Sharpeners under his control.

'Because of this new development, we must act quickly,' he told them. 'The children of Franz Schubert School must be transported to Planet Z13, along with their Headmaster, as soon as possible, before the children of Chivvy Chase School can cause any trouble. Some of them are natural troublemakers, and although I hope they have forgotten about us, I don't want to take any chances. Also, I think it would be helpful if we had the lady in charge of them under our control if possible, if only to keep her quiet while the operation is under way. If the opportunity arises, bring her to me!'

So when Spiky, the policeman and Mrs Somervil set off into the woods, the junior Brain Sharpeners pressed switches and beamed rays enthusiastically, with the result that a pepperpot craft was ready to receive her when she walked alone by the pond.

Whether it was an accident that she chose to walk by the path and not with Spiky and the policeman through the trees, or whether the Brain Sharpeners were already influencing her, is a riddle to this day. The fact is that she walked almost without stopping, straight into the craft, and in no time was standing before the Commander.

The Brain Sharpeners hadn't much experience in dealing with women, and their language expert had to advise the Commander on the best way of addressing Inge Somervil.

'Madam,' he began, 'will you please explain how it is that the children of Chivvy Chase School have suddenly appeared in Bad Unterfeld? Why are they here, and what are they doing?'

'I have an excellent answer to that question,' replied Mrs Somervil, showing that nothing in or out of this world could easily upset her. 'But first of all, where do you come from and why are you here?'

The Commander decided he had better reply or he might not make much progress with her.

'We are Brain Sharpeners from Outer Space,' he explained, 'and we are here to improve the brains of the human race and help it to develop.'

He didn't say where it was intended the humans should go after their development.

'Oh, that is nice,' answered Inge Somervil, looking at him out of blue Nordic eyes, and smiling attractive-

ly. 'I am all in favour of understanding between races, wherever they may come from. Now I can answer your questions. The children of Chivvy Chase School are here because I want to encourage friendship between nations, particularly between the children of my own nation and those of my husband's.'

The Brain Sharpener looked a bit puzzled.

'You see, I was born in Bad Unterfeld,' explained Inge, 'and my husband lives at Chivvy Chase. My daughter goes to Chivvy Chase School, so I thought it was a splendid opportunity to help bring the two towns together. I arranged for Chivvy Chase to be twinned with Bad Unterfeld, so that visits could be made. Don't you agree that it's a good idea?'

The Commander waited for the translation of her words to be completed, then waited a little longer to try and make head or tail of what she was talking about. Brain Sharpeners are Brain Sharpeners all over their planet, and so it was difficult for him to understand that people on the same planet needed to be brought together in order to be friends. But being a Brain Sharpener, he quickly found the right approach.

'So you would be happy if the children of Franz Schubert School took a trip into space?' he asked.

'Why, yes, of course,' replied Mrs Somervil. 'What could be nicer! And if the children of Chivvy Chase School could go with them—'

'We don't want them!' declared the Commander bluntly. 'How long are they staying in Bad Unterfeld?'

'Only a few days more,' said Mrs Somervil. 'I hope to arrange a return visit soon—'

'Never mind that!' growled the Commander. 'Do you promise to help the Headmaster to arrange this visit for us?'

91

'Oh yes—how exciting!'

'And you will also help keep the children of Chivvy Chase away from the woods around Bad Unterfeld at all times?'

'All right, if you wish. But really, you are missing a great chance to improve understanding—'

The Commander pressed a switch and spoke into his visiphone.

'Take her away!' he ordered. 'Return her to Earth at once.'

'But—don't you wish her to be brain sharpened?' asked the Brain Sharpener at the other end.

'No, I don't. I think it would take too long. She acts already as if she were the centre of this universe! Besides, she's quite prepared to help us. Thinks we're going to let the little humans become our friends. Ha, ha, ha!'

The laughter of the Commander was not pleasant to hear. It was already dark when Mrs Somervil was landed back by the pond. She drew her shawl more tightly around her shoulders and set off as fast as she could for the Headmaster's house.

There, to her surprise, she was greeted by not only the Headmaster but by Mr Browser, Helmut's father and her own daughter.

'Oh Mummy! Where have you been?' cried little Inga, running to embrace her mother.

'What a relief that you're back,' said Mr Browser.

'We were thinking of sending a search party out for you. Whatever happened?'

Inge Somervil now had to think quickly. They were all looking at her very hard, especially the policeman, and she decided against telling the truth, in case Mr Browser became suspicious and the policeman thought she was going out of her mind.

'You shouldn't have worried, all of you,' she said. 'I just lost myself in the woods, and when I found the right path again it was already dark.'

'Are you sure that's correct?' asked the policeman in German. 'I thought I saw something quite different happen. You seemed to disappear in a cloud of dust.'

'There was a sudden rush of wind, and something went in my eye, and I took cover amongst the trees for a while. Then I saw you had gone, and I went for a walk—and lost myself.'

The policeman shook his head in disbelief, but the Headmaster decided to give her his support.

'I see no reason to disbelieve what Frau Somervil has said,' he declared. 'I don't accept for one moment what you have been talking about, Herr Schneider.'

'So much for the Brain Sharpeners,' said Mr Browser, relieved.

'I must take Inga home to bed,' said Mrs Somervil. 'I'm sorry to have been so much of a nuisance to you all. I won't keep you any longer. Goodnight.'

'She is not speaking the truth,' persisted Helmut's

93

father when she had gone. 'If you had seen what we saw, Herr Browser, you would know that your Brain Sharpeners have come back. The boy Simon Jackson told me all about them.'

'Herr Schneider, please do not talk nonsense,' said the Headmaster. 'Mr Browser and I will play a game of chess, and then we shall retire to bed early. I have a most busy day tomorrow. I am going to take Class S out to the woods in the afternoon for a fitness walk—'

'A fitness walk! Ach—no! I will go now, Herr Weissmann—but Herr Browser, I would most like to speak with you before I go.'

Mr Browser went to the door with him, in spite of the disapproving look from the Headmaster. Outside on the pavement the policeman turned to speak.

'All I have said is true, Herr Browser, I swear it! And now it seems that tomorrow afternoon my boy may disappear into space. Already these creatures have Frau Somervil on their side. Please, I beg you, don't let it happen! I see it all so clearly now—these poor children and their Headmaster are to be taken as slaves. Say you will come and try and stop them, please!'

Mr Browser put his hand on the policeman's arm, and spoke in his best German.

'I am on your side, Herr Schneider, don't worry! I dare not let Herr Weissmann know what I now believe, or he may do something foolish. Tomorrow we will do our best to defy the Brain Sharpeners—but now I shall play chess with Herr Weissmann, and I shall lose!'

He winked at Herr Schneider and turned back into the house.

'Thank heavens I'm not alone,' said the policeman, and walked home with his hand on the revolver he had brought with him, as though he feared the Brain Sharpeners might suddenly come to get him.

Mr Browser played two games of chess and lost them both—perhaps because his mind was on the Brain Sharpeners, or perhaps because the sharpened brain of the Headmaster was too quick for him.

'I shall now have a drink and go to bed,' said the Headmaster, standing up and offering Mr Browser his hand. 'I have a busy day tomorrow.'

'So have I,' said Mr Browser as he shook hands. The Headmaster smiled at him pityingly, as he did when children told some made-up story.

'Sleep well,' he said. 'Goodnight.'

'Goodnight,' replied Mr Browser—but he didn't sleep at all well. Thoughts of the Brain Sharpeners plagued him all night long.

6

Shocks all Round

On the next morning Spiky was as keen to go to school as Helmut was—but for a very different reason. He wanted to be there early in order to contact Anna and the rest of his friends and tell them what had happened on the previous evening. Selwyn was the first to arrive, and Spiky was glad about this because he knew that at least Selwyn would listen to him.

Selwyn listened, and when he had finished speaking Spiky waited anxiously to hear what Selwyn thought. If he couldn't convince Selwyn, thought Spiky, there wasn't much hope with many of the others.

'I believe you're right,' said Selwyn earnestly. 'All the signs are that Class S is being controlled by the Brain Sharpeners—and their Headmaster, too. And if Inga's mother is on their side as well, we shall have to look out for our own safety. She's bossy enough, without having the Brain Sharpeners to help her. But perhaps nothing will happen before we go home—'

'I wouldn't like Class S to become the slaves of the Brain Sharpeners,' put in Spiky. 'We are the only ones who could warn them.'

'They won't take any notice of us,' declared Selwyn, shaking his head. 'Who have we on our side?'

'Maybe Mr Browser, and certainly Herr Schneider, the policeman.'

'German policemen carry guns,' said Selwyn thoughtfully.

'You don't imagine the Brain Sharpeners would let him shoot them, do you?' commented Spiky.

'I suppose not,' agreed Selwyn, still thoughtful. 'Here come some of the others.'

'I'll speak to Anna first,' said Spiky, 'because she won't need persuading. She saw the Headmaster disappear. Then the three of us will have to speak to as many of the class as possible.'

Anna Cardwell heard Spiky's report of what had happened to Mrs Somervil.

'Of course I believe it happened,' she told him. 'But what can we do about it? I tried to make Astrid understand the danger she's in, but she just looked at me as if I was crazy. They're all in the power of the Brain Sharpeners, and there's not much we can do about it.'

Michael Fairlie knew the truth, but he was unwilling to admit it.

'Maybe you're right,' he told Spiky, 'but I've had enough to do with the Brain Sharpeners. I don't want to be mixed up with them any more.'

The rest of the class, their memories of their earlier brushes with the Brain Sharpeners dimmed, listened politely but clearly wished they hadn't been told.

Their minds were more on their return home in a few days' time, for although they had enjoyed their visit, a little bit of homesickness was creeping in, and they were looking forward to English food and English tea. Anna Cardwell came up against complete disbelief when she talked to Inga Somervil.

'Your mother probably thinks the Brain Sharpeners are friendly,' said Anna, 'but they're not! They'll kidnap all of Class S, and Herr Weissmann, and if she's not careful they'll take her as well.'

'Rubbish!' replied Inga, shaking her fair curls like her mother did when she was annoyed or excited. 'My mother knows what she's doing, and as for all this talk of Brain Sharpeners, I've never heard such nonsense. I think you're mad because Class S are all working hard—that's my opinion.'

'And it's your mother's as well,' said Anna, annoyed.

While Class 8 and Class S were being given a joint English and German lesson by Fräulein Schmidt and Mr Caracco, Herr Weissmann called Mr Browser and Mrs Somervil to his room.

'I am afraid there must be a change in our plans today,' he said in his precise English. 'I know that we were planning to have a sports afternoon together, but that will not now take place. I have to take Class S with me to the wood, to complete their study of local plants before their examinations.'

'I thought it was to keep them fit—' put in Mr Browser, but Herr Weissmann ignored him.

'That's quite understood, Herr Weissmann,' said Mrs Somervil brightly. 'You will take your children for an extra swimming afternoon, won't you, Mr Browser—and I would like to come with you, Herr Weissmann.'

Now Mr Browser didn't much like being told exactly what to do, even by his own wife. He was feeling hot enough about Herr Weissmann's excuse to hide the truth that he wanted to take Class S to meet the Brain Sharpeners again—and Inge Somervil's words made him boil over.

'I will decide for myself, Mrs Somervil,' he declared. 'And Herr Weissmann, perhaps it's time I told you that I know the truth. You are taking your children to the Brain Sharpeners, and without realising it you are leading them into great danger. Draw back, Herr Weissmann, before it is too late. Slavery in Outer Space is all the Brain Sharpeners will offer you—perhaps even today they will carry you all off, never to return!'

Herr Weissmann half closed his blue eyes and stared at Mr Browser.

'What is all this about?' he asked.

'Do not listen to him, Herr Weissmann,' put in Mrs Somervil. 'These stories of hostile creatures from other worlds are the product of the wild ideas of some of Mr Browser's children. Take no notice of him!'

'I thought so—you are under the influence as well,' said Mr Browser. 'I warn you, Herr Weissmann, if you assist the Brain Sharpeners, the whole world may soon be at risk—'

'Mr Browser, I have heard enough. I do not wish to know any more about the strange ideas of your children. I must remind you that you are visitors here in Bad Unterfeld, and that the children of Franz Schubert School and what they do does not concern you at all. They are under my control.'

'But it is my concern—' protested Mr Browser. Herr Weissmann pushed his arms out wide to show he didn't want to discuss the matter further.

'Frau Somervil, please arrange with the swimming pool for Mr Browser's children to enter as a group this afternoon,' he said.

'I will do that at once, Herr Weissmann,' said Inga's mother, and the meeting was over.

During the morning it was the custom for the English children to meet together with their teachers to discuss any difficulties they had. At this meeting Mr Browser revealed the change of plan which the Head-master had introduced.

'But sir!' called out Spiky Jackson. 'You know what that means! Either they are going to have their brains further sharpened, or they are going to be carried off!'

'Quiet, Simon!' ordered Mr Caracco, but Mr Browser looked disturbed.

'I would like you children to write up your diaries now,' he said, 'while I talk to Mr Caracco. Selwyn, what is it you want?'

Selwyn was standing beside Mr Browser with his hand held high in the air.

'No need to hold your hand up like that,' went on Mr Browser. 'What's worrying you, boy?'

'Please, Mr Browser, if the Brain Sharpeners are going to carry off Class S, we'll have to use all the help

101

we can in order to stop them, won't we!'

'Of course,' agreed Mr Browser. 'If the Brain Sharpeners really are about, it's a highly dangerous situation, but I can hardly believe they are. I thought they had gone away into space—'

'No, they're back, Mr Browser, and Helmut Schneider's father, the policeman, saw them, so he's on our side.'

'Indeed,' said Mr Browser. 'I suppose it's good to have the police on one's side, but I don't see what help he can be against creatures like the Brain Sharpeners!'

'He's armed, Mr Browser. He carries a gun.'

'Thank you for the information, Selwyn. Now I should forget all about it and sit down and write your diary. I wish to talk to Mr Caracco.'

Selwyn was so disappointed that his lower jaw dropped and he looked with pleading eyes at Mr Browser.

'You heard what Mr Browser said,' put in Mr Caracco, and that was the end of it. Selwyn dejectedly made his way back to his seat. Mr Browser did talk with Mr Caracco, and very earnestly, but nobody else could hear what was said. At the end of the conversation, Mr Caracco left in order to have a word with Fräulein Schmidt, and when he returned Anna Cardwell was able to overhear what he said.

'Herr Weissmann is leaving with the children from here at three o'clock,' he said. 'I must say that Sigrid

Schmidt is very unhappy about what is going on in her class. She says they're not the same children as they used to be—they're much cleverer, but not nearly as pleasant nor as happy.'

'There you are,' said Mr Browser. 'I shall be leaving the school now, and you will continue until the end of school with Mr Caracco. This afternoon you will all meet at the swimming pool at half past two. You will have to go on your own, because Class S have to report back to school. You know the way to the pool—if you aren't sure, go with someone who does know the way. Take care, and don't be late.'

'If we don't want to swim, Mr Browser, do we have to?' called out Selwyn.

Selwyn, in his way, was just as big a nuisance as more mischievous boys like Spiky and Michael Fairlie, thought Mr Browser.

'No, I suppose not, Selwyn,' he said. 'You can watch the others, if that's what you prefer.'

When Mr Browser had gone, Selwyn took the opportunity to move across to talk to Spiky.

'Don't despair,' he said. 'Browser is up to something. Otherwise he would have said I had to go swimming, like all the rest. Maybe none of us is going swimming really.'

'Don't kid yourself,' replied Spiky—and Mr Caracco closed the conversation by telling everybody to listen to him.

In fact, Mr Browser left the school and made straight for Bad Unterfeld police station, which was a small and quiet building, because nearly all the citizens of Bad Unterfeld were very law abiding. There he talked to Herr Schneider for a while before going back to Herr Weissmann's house for lunch. The Headmaster was very nervous and said little, avoiding Mr Browser's eyes as if afraid to be drawn into an awkward conversation, and Mr Browser was pleased when the meal was over and he could escape. He arrived early at the swimming pool, and drank a coffee in the restaurant while he waited.

It was not long afterwards when the sound of scuffling and high-pitched voices told him that some of his charges were on the scene. Anxious not to be the cause of a disturbance outside the calm waters of the Bad Unterfeld swimming pool, he hurriedly paid his bill and joined the gathering in the impressive entrance hall.

'Line up quietly on the pavement outside,' ordered Mr Browser.

'But Mr Browser, we're going inside—' protested Angela. 'Can't we line up here?'

'Do as you're told!' demanded Mr Browser in his sternest tones, and so they obeyed.

'Spiky Jackson isn't here yet,' called out Michael Fairlie.'I heard him say he had better things to do.'

'Indeed,' said Mr Browser, frowning. 'He had

nothing to do which could be more important than what we are about to do!'

'What's that, Mr Browser?' asked Jason Little.

'You'll see, Jason,' replied Mr Browser. 'Ah—I see that Simon Jackson is here after all.'

Spiky came running, panting for breath.

'Where've you been, Spiky?' called out Anna.

'I didn't want to come,' said Spiky, but in the end Helmut's father persuaded me. 'You could have told us what's going on, Mr Browser!'

Mr Browser thought of telling him off, but changed his mind.

'I didn't have time,' he said. 'Now, make twos and follow me.'

'But what about our swim, Mr Browser?' objected Inga Somervil when she saw he was heading away from the pool.

'We might go swimming later, Inga,' replied Mr Browser mysteriously. 'By the way, where's your mother?'

'She said she'd rather go with the Headmaster and his party,' replied Inga. 'And if we're not going swimming, I would rather have gone with them to the woods too.'

'Don't worry,' said Mr Browser. 'We're going to the woods as well.'

'Why, Mr Browser?'

'It's the Brain Sharpeners,' whispered Selwyn to

Anna. 'Maybe he's going to try and stop them.'

'But it's crazy to take us near them.'

'They won't want us,' said Selwyn calmly. 'They're after Class S. They've sharpened their brains, not ours. We're just a nuisance to them.'

'I hope so,' said Anna doubtfully.

They walked in the direction of the woods, some of them murmuring complaints about not being able to have a swim, so that in the end Mr Browser tried to pacify them.

'When we've finished what we have to do, maybe we'll have time for you to swim afterwards,' he told them.

At the point where the road ended and the path into the woods began, three people were waiting for them. One was Herr Schneider, who was in uniform, and whose police car was parked at the end of the road. The other two were Mr Caracco and Fräulein Schmidt, who looked as though she had only just stopped crying.

'We are all here,' Mr Browser told the policeman, 'except for Mrs Somervil, who preferred to go with Herr Weissmann.'

'Yes, yes,' replied the policeman, as if he had expected Inga's mother to have made that choice.

'Oh, Mr Browser, my poor class,' burst out Fräulein Schmidt. 'Mr Caracco has told me terrible things of them. They cannot surely be true?'

106

'Come with us, and we will see,' said Mr Browser grimly. 'Herr Schneider, you are now in charge. We will follow you.'

'Do not be afraid, children,' said Herr Schneider, taking out his gun. 'I will not point this at you.'

The presence of a gun, whether it is pointed at you or not, is enough to quieten most people, and Class 8 looked at the gun, then at Mr Browser, and were silent. The policeman waved to them to follow him, and walked quietly along the path. The sound of their feet was deadened by the pine needles that covered the ground.

'Surely he can't think that he can frighten the Brain Sharpeners off with one gun?' whispered Spiky.

'Maybe he doesn't want to frighten them,' said Selwyn. Alison Gilpin had overheard what Spiky had said, and something stirred in the depths of her memory.

'Brain Sharpeners? We aren't going anywhere near them, are we? Anna, do you remember, something happened once at school, and we had a narrow escape. Where is Mr Browser taking us this time? Have they got him in their power again? I'm not going any further—I'm frightened! These woods are so dark and gloomy, anything could happen!'

And Alison stood still. Several others, having heard what she had said, hesitated as well, and Mr Browser saw that he might soon have a mutiny on his hands.

'Just a little further,' he said, 'and then we shall stop. We are going to wait for a while in the woods until Class S come this way. Herr Weissmann's children are in danger, and we are here to try to save them from trouble.'

'What trouble, Mr Browser?' called out someone.

'How thick some people are!' muttered Spiky. 'Even after we tried to warn them, they still don't want to know about the Brain Sharpeners.'

Helmut's father waved them on, and because Alison and a few others were not keen to wander about on their own in a foreign country, they preferred to stay with the party. Soon the policeman stopped and waved for them to leave the path and hide behind the trees on the edge of the wood.

'Spread out,' ordered Mr Browser, 'and when Class S appears, stop them from going into the woods. There is a pond lying behind us, and there is the danger. Whatever they say, stop them going through, even if Herr Weissmann tells them to!'

The policeman nodded to show that he understood the meaning of what Mr Browser had been saying, and he too hid behind a tree.

'*Sie kommen*!' he called out in a low voice. 'They come!'

Class S came marching through the wood in twos, like a well-drilled army, with Herr Weissmann at the front and Mrs Somervil at the rear.

'Halt!' ordered Herr Weissmann, and pointing into the woods, added something else in German. Then he stepped forward, to lead them into the trees. At the same time, from the direction of the pond came a whirring sound which Class 8 had heard before, and which struck terror in them.

'The Brain Sharpeners!' whispered Spiky. 'They're there!'

'It sounds as though there's a tornado somewhere,' said Inga Somervil, puzzled by the fear in her companions' faces. Herr Weissmann impatiently waved Class S on again.

Out of the trees stepped Mr Browser. 'Don't go any further!' he begged Herr Weissmann, stretching his arms out wide to include the children. 'You'll all be carried away!'

The Headmaster looked at him in surprise and annoyance, and couldn't be bothered to translate his thoughts into English. He tried to push Mr Browser to one side, and urged Class S on yet again. Mrs Somervil came to his side.

'What's the matter, Mr Browser?' she demanded, annoyed. 'Why are you stopping us? We have to go to the pond. Come, children!'

She spoke the last words in German, and tried to move off the path with the Headmaster. Astrid and Siegfried, Helmut and some others tried to follow, all looking most earnest and determined.

'Stop!' Suddenly Helmut's father appeared—and he was pointing his gun straight at Herr Weissmann. He added a sharp order in German which even Class 8 understood to mean 'Stand still, or I shoot!'

Class S and Mrs Somervil stopped in surprise, just as they were about to fight their way through the ranks of Class 8. They were mostly shocked by the sight of their Headmaster being threatened by a policeman, a happening which threw their minds into confusion and for a few seconds even overcame the power of the Brain Sharpeners. The effect was even stronger on the Headmaster. He stared at the gun and at Herr Schneider in his uniform, and he could not believe what was happening. The call of the Brain Sharpeners was strong, but to be challenged by the arm of the law for the first time in his correct life was completely upsetting. Herr Weissmann had always stood for justice and correctness, and now he was flung into confusion.

The only person who was not overcome was Mrs Somervil.

'Let me go and tell them what has happened,' she said. 'It is time we were due to meet them. I'll tell them we can't come today.'

'Don't go!' begged Mr Browser.

'Mummy, let me come too!' pleaded Inga.

'You can't!' declared Mr Browser, grabbing her.

Mrs Somervil thrust two of the Class 8 girls aside.

'I can't shoot a woman!' said the policeman in English. 'Let her go!'

'The Brain Sharpeners will have her!' called out Michael Fairlie, but Mr Browser had already decided that he would prefer to risk one person than a number of the children.

Class S made no attempt to follow her—they were still looking to their Headmaster for orders, and he was hiding his face in his hands, as though what was happening was too much for him. Inga started to cry, Anna held her hand.

They heard the footsteps of Mrs Somervil as she passed between the trees. The area of the pond was now silent, and Anna and Spiky tried to calculate how long it would take Mrs Somervil to reach the Brain Sharpeners.

Then the whirring and hissing sound began again, and grew and grew in strength until children were putting their hands to their ears.

'Aa—aah!' There was a long drawn out scream, followed by a splash, and then a cloud formed in the sky above them, rose up and disappeared.

'We must help her!' cried Mr Browser, though secretly he believed Mrs Somervil was gone with the Brain Sharpeners for good. They all scrambled between the trees, and when the view of the pond burst upon them they saw nothing at first.

'The Brain Sharpeners have gone!' cried Anna.

'There she is!' cried Inga. 'Look—in the water!'

Mrs Somervil's head broke the surface of the water, and she floundered there like some stricken porpoise. Without any hesitation Helmut's father rushed to the pond, threw off his jacket and waded out to her. Only for the last few metres did he have to swim, and he quickly pulled her back into shallow water and landed her, gasping on the bank.

After Inga had been reunited with her mother, and Herr Weissmann had put his jacket over the dripping lady, she recovered enough to speak.

'Those Brain Sharpeners,' she said, 'were waiting for me, with the door of their space craft standing open. Dust was flying all around, and I was almost choking when I reached the door. I felt I had to tell them what had happened, so I said I was sorry but we had been delayed—'

'Did you tell them by whom?' asked Mr Browser.

'Yes—and then it all happened. I said that Mr Browser and his children had stopped Herr Weissmann, and that they knew who the Brain Sharpeners were. Then I heard strange voices, and suddenly there came a great whirring noise, and as I moved nearer to the door a huge blast of air hit me, the door closed, and I was flung right into the middle of the pond. And now the Brain Sharpeners seem to have gone.'

'My dear Mrs Somervil, they have,' said Mr Browser, 'and you have had the narrowest escape of any

113

human being for a long time.'

'I don't understand them,' said Mrs Somervil, wringing out her skirt. 'I was only trying to be friendly.'

'My good Mrs Somervil,' said Herr Weissmann, who had by now recovered somewhat from his shock, 'no doubt you meant well—but we were all being tricked by these creatures. I see it all now—they had us in their power, and made us work and work, not for our own good. Mr Browser, I shake hands with you, and with Herr Schneider. You are an excellent example to the German police.'

'To the police of all the world,' said Mr Browser.

'And I hope you can begin to forgive us for our behaviour,' went on Herr Weissmann. 'We did not know what we were doing.'

'Oh dear, and I only meant to be friendly,' repeated Mrs Somervil, sniffing.

'There is a time for everything,' said Herr Weissmann. 'And it is clear that it is not yet time for us to make friends with hostile creatures from Outer Space. Let us be content that we are all friends here on Earth!'

'Hear hear!' added Mr Browser, surprised by the change in the Headmaster's manner.

'And tomorrow,' said the Headmaster, turning to the children, 'there will be no work done. It will be a holiday, and we will swim, and have picnics, run races and play games.'

He repeated the message in German, but it was really unnecessary, for the cheering from Class 8 had given Class S an idea of what was going on. Helmut and his friends stood there undecided, slow to follow their Headmaster out of the spell under which he had put them. Herr Weissmann was like a man from whom a great burden had been lifted. He spoke with the policeman in German.

'I think it would be best not to tell people too much about what has happened today. I shall certainly report how you bravely saved the life of Frau Somervil. Beyond that, we need not go. Do you agree?'

The policeman looked at the laughing, playing children—including some of Class S, now fast recovering—and he agreed. After all, what good would it have done him to try and tell his fellow officers that he had helped fight off an attempt to kidnap children by some creatures called Brain Sharpeners? No doubt they would have laughed their heads off, and perhaps sent him away for a few weeks for what is called a cure.

'I'm not doing any work at all tonight,' said Helmut on the way home. 'Spiky—you help me with my model train?'

Spiky was taken by surprise at being called by his nickname, but he could see from the smile on Helmut's face that he had changed from being a solemn automaton and had become a normal boy again—a change which extended to all the rest of Class S, who if possible made more noise as they walked back through the woods than did Class 8.

Fräulein Schmidt, when she realised what had happened, was near to tears of joy, and had to be comforted by Mr Caracco.

7

Return Journeys

The sports and picnic afternoon organised at short notice by Herr Weissmann, Sigrid Schmidt and, of course, Inge Somervil, was a great success, especially as it was backed up by plenty of ice cream and cold drinks.

Helmut's father found time to join them for half an hour, and caused a sensation by starting the hundred metres race with the same gun with which he had threatened the Headmaster.

Spiky Jackson, perhaps because he was again free of worry about the Brain Sharpeners, won the hundred metres, and perhaps for the same reason Anna Cardwell, much to her surprise, jumped higher than anyone else. Most of the other events were won by Class S, perhaps because they were so happy at last to be free from everlasting work. Spiky watched Helmut winning the long jump in surprise and admiration.

'Look at him, Mike—this is the first time he's been interested in anything except swotting!'

Class 8 children were beginning to lose the feeling of being inferior now that they could see Class S enjoying themselves just like any other ordinary human beings. Both classes cheered themselves hoarse during the Staff Sack Race, during which Herr Weissmann fell over and spent the rest of the race sitting there laughing, while Mr Browser was unable to make his sack move more than one inch at a time. The result was a tie between Mr Caracco and Fräulein Schmidt, but only because Mr Caracco fell over when he was about to cross the line and couldn't get up until Fräulein Schmidt reached him.

At the end of it all Spiky went home with Helmut, who was trying to make conversation about all kinds of subjects he had never mentioned before.

'Have you seen ever a handball game?' he asked. 'Bad Unterfeld plays a team from the big town of Drefeld tonight, and if my father becomes tickets, we shall go.'

Spiky was too polite to smile at Helmut's funny English, because he knew his own German was limited to about four words. When they had eaten the salad and pizza prepared by Helmut's mother, Helmut easily persuaded his father to take them to the match.

'Must you not work, Helmut?' asked his mother in surprise.

'No, I've done enough work to last me for a long time,' Helmut answered her, and for Spiky's benefit added in English: 'Too much work—no good!' with which Spiky at once agreed. Helmut's mother was upset at first, but when the boys and her husband had gone to watch the handball, she sat down in front of

the television set, which was showing the German translation of 'Dallas', and reflected that after all she didn't much like work herself, so she couldn't expect too much of her son.

The next few days passed quickly in holiday spirit, and in no time Class 8 were standing on the platform at Bad Unterfeld station again, waiting to start their journey home. There was no band to see them off, because most of the bandsmen couldn't be spared from their jobs, but there were speeches from Herr Weissmann and Mr Browser, and promises on all sides that Class S should visit Chivvy Chase in the future. This idea was much applauded by Mr Caracco and Fräulein Schmidt, and by Mrs Somervil, who was rapidly recovering from the shock of being put in the pond by the Brain Sharpeners.

With the humans all happy again, perhaps a thought can be spared for the Brain Sharpeners, shooting back into space and once more robbed of the chance to carry off some little human slaves. The Prime Brain Sharpener was most annoyed with the Commander for failing again, and as a punishment banished him to Planet Z13, where an expeditionary force was trying to prove that the climate of the planet was suitable for Brain Sharpeners to survive in and develop. As the temperature was never less than one hundred degrees, the fate of Class S would have been most unpleasant but for the arrival of Spiky and Anna in Bad Unterfeld. The Brain Sharpeners still hope to come across some species in space which will do their dirty work in developing their spare planet for them, for the number of Sharpeners on their own planet increases so fast that it is badly overcrowded already. The situation could become so grave that the Prime Brain Sharpener may change his tactics and decide to put his surplus population on Earth; secretly the Commander hopes that he will be put in charge of the invasion, when it comes. Maybe the Prime Brain Sharpener is waiting for the humans to be so busy quarrelling amongst themselves that he can send his Sharpeners down without anybody noticing.

Meanwhile the members of Class 8 and Class S are writing letters to one another when they can find the time. The letters are mostly in English, except those written by Inga Somervil, whose mother makes her write in German.

But there are rumours that one or two of the children have bought German phrase books, and are looking forward to learning languages at their Comprehensive School. One thing is certain—Mr Caracco is studying hard, going to German classes twice a week, and even saying a few German words to Fräulein Schmidt on the telephone when he rings her.

Mr Browser is just happy that everyone came home safely, and that the Brain Sharpeners appear to have been forgotten again.

'Well, George,' said Mr Sage to him one day when Mr Browser was on his way to his classroom, 'do you think you learned much on the trip to Bad Unterfeld? As a party, I mean.'

'Oh, yes,' replied Mr Browser. 'The children learned that they can't speak German, Mrs Somervil learned that you can't make friends with everybody all at once, and Mr Caracco learned much to his advantage.'

It was a funny answer, not the sort Mr Sage had expected, and the Headmaster gave Mr Browser one of his suspicious looks.

'And what did you learn?' he asked.

'I learned that I like egg and bacon for breakfast much more than rolls and butter and jam,' said Mr Browser.

The Headmaster walked away, shaking his head.

When would George Browser learn to say the right thing at the right time?

As for Mr Browser, he went into his classroom and immediately said the right thing.

'Anna Cardwell and Simon Jackson—stop playing about and get down to work,' he said.

And Class 8 knew he meant the rest of them as well. Life was normal again at Chivvy Chase School.

Other Titles in Andersen Young Readers' Library

Pamela Blackie	*Jinny the Witch Flies Over the House*
Roger Collinson	*Get Lavinia Goodbody!*
	Paper Flags and Penny Ices
Philip Curtis	*A Gift from Another Galaxy*
	A Party for Lester
	Bewitched by the Brain Sharpeners
	Mr Browser and the Brain Sharpeners
	Mr Browser and the Comet Crisis
	Mr Browser and the Mini-Meteorites
	Mr Browser in the Space Museum
	The Quest of the Quidnuncs
	The Revenge of the Brain Sharpeners
	The Toothless Wonder in the Tower
Nigel Hinton	*Run to Beaver Towers*

J. K. Hooper	*Kaspar and the Iron Poodle*
Julia Jarman	*Ollie and the Bogle* *When Poppy Ran Away*
Pat McAughey	*Lost Emerald*
John Singleton	*The Adventures of Muckpup*
Brenda Sivers	*Biminy in Danger*
Angela Sommer-Bodenburg	*The Little Vampire* *The Little Vampire in Love* *The Little Vampire Moves In* *The Little Vampire on the* *Farm* *The Little Vampire Takes a* *Trip*
Robert Taylor	*The Line of Dunes*
David Tinkler	*The Headmaster Went Splat!* *The Scourge of the Dinner* *Ladies* *The Snoots Strike Back*
Hazel Townson	*Danny—Don't Jump!* *Haunted Ivy* *One Green Bottle* *Pilkie's Progress* *The Choking Peril* *The Great Ice-Cream Crime* *The Shrieking Face*

125